A
SACK
HALF
FULL

FROM HUMILITY TO HUMOR

JERRY DUPREZ

A
SACK
HALF
FULL

FROM HUMILITY TO HUMOR

One Family's

Journey through

Testicular Cancer

TATE PUBLISHING
AND ENTERPRISES, LLC

Published by Tate Publishing & Enterprises, LLC
127 E. Trade Center Terrace | Mustang, Oklahoma 73064 USA
1.888.361.9473 | www.tatepublishing.com

Tate Publishing is committed to excellence in the publishing industry. The company reflects the philosophy established by the founders, based on Psalm 68:11,
"The Lord gave the word and great was the company of those who published it."

Book design copyright © 2011 by Tate Publishing, LLC. All rights reserved.
Cover design by Kenna Davis
Interior design by Christina Hicks

Published in the United States of America

ISBN: 978-1-61346-723-7
1. Biography & Autobiography / Personal Memoirs
2. Health & Fitness / Diseases / Cancer
12.01.18

To Denel (my soulmate, my Caramia, my Dulcinea Del Toboso, and the best nurse); Harry (my mentor and friend); and Dody J. (the "Babe Ruth" of cancer survival). And to all my children: Belinda, Nicole, Chris, Gabe and Angel...and their children, and their children...

TABLE OF CONTENTS

INTRODUCTION

For me, some of the realities of testicular cancer, beyond the pain and fear, were too funny to make up. I took notes throughout the process because the humor kept coming; from the names of doctors, the many humbling indignities, and some unique experiences, it seemed like a natural fit for a stand-up comedy routine. A friend, Malorie, suggested to my wife that I write a book. Now I have been blessed with many gifts, skills, and talents but discerning the will of God is certainly not one of them, at least to date.

Having the idea for a book arise from another person—a godly person at that—gave me pause. Maybe this was a plan to follow. After all, I am probably a better writer than a performer anyway. I asked my daughter, Nikki, and wife, Denel, to pray about it. By the time one week had passed, the book had flowed out of me. The rough draft was complete and ready for review. I asked those reviewing it to consider three questions as they read: 1) Did you laugh? 2) Were you uplifted, encouraged? 3) Does it violate any Christian tenet; is it edifying? This last question was relevant because, despite my education and beliefs, there was one swear/cuss word that best described part of this whole experience. It just fit too perfectly not to use it. But I was also aware that it might offend some. I am a Christian and, in my mind, this book should appeal to Christians and non-Christians alike. I write, however well or poorly, from an honest and pretty raw perspective. I didn't hold back in this book. But it is raw enough where I could see some people being taken aback at times as they read. The last thing I want in my authenticity is to even dance the lines of being sacrilegious (no pun intended). If Grandma picked it up at a Christian bookstore, I could imagine some shock at the cuss word used and possibly the rawness as well, as she asked her husband, "Honey, what are blue balls?" So I don't know where this book will end up. It really belongs in both Christian and secular bookstores in the "Immature/Raw/Authentic" section. Unfortunately (or fortunately, depending on your point of view), no such section currently exists.

I read most of Lance Armstrong's book about testicular cancer, *It's Not About the Bike: My Journey Back to Life*. It was full of information and hope and was a great help. However, as chemotherapy progressed, there came a point where I couldn't read it anymore. Everything during chemo, even the few meals that I regularly ate, came to be associated with that season of my life. The sensory and emotional correlations between various things and the chemo got somehow stuck in my very being and thus needed to be actively avoided, at least for a time. Lance's book is a great gift, and his foundation has done amazing things to help thousands of people deal with some hard realities. But at one point, I could no longer read about testicular cancer. I was living it in all its horrible glory. The path of treatment was too thorny. I needed a spiritual deepening and comic relief desperately. This book, together with Lance's, will hopefully give that to you or a loved one, if you need that. It is also meant to echo the openness that is found in women's approach to breast cancer. Some things are hard to talk about and very personal, but their openness is a good model for men to follow with colon, prostate, testicular, and other cancers. Confronting denial and actively addressing issues is arguably a tougher but ultimately much healthier path, both physically and emotionally. This is a truth with applications throughout our lives.

I sometimes think I'm a pretty smart guy. I have even accomplished some things. Together, I can be pretty prideful. However, God has richly blessed me with humbling experiences throughout my life. My head can never get too puffed up before, *wham!* Reality hits, and I know again my smallness in things. This book chronicles a rather rich set of humbling indignities I "enjoyed" during my treatment process for testicular cancer. I hope they make you laugh, deepen your relationship with God, and encourage you and yours.

Regarding the rawness of the book at times, my intended audience is adult, all males, and approximately half the female population. Of the latter, I'm thinking of those who can handle and possibly even enjoy some raw male humor and honesty. This book is not for everyone. Before we let a few close friends review it, we gave a copy to each of our kids (all young adults). If they felt it was too raw or personal, they had a veto on the whole project. Unfortunately, because it hit so close to home for them, reading it was very slow and painful at times. The process was reliving the whole ordeal and, although it certainly was a joyful outcome, too much of an emotional roller coaster for them. We decided to proceed without their review. They have the manuscript for posterity. As a side note, since the chapter on sex is especially open and raw, feel free to skip it if you wish. However, for veteran couples, married for twenty-plus years, I've received very positive feedback. A particular couple, married for over twenty-five years, said, "It was true to that season of life, hysterical and hilarious." Proceed at your own risk/enjoyment.

I've struggled often with the title of this book. I've been told by knowledgeable people, and intuitively felt myself, that it isn't wise to have a title that many people would have to overcome to explore further. It might be a speed bump for some and a roadblock for others. However, the title fit with the experience and was framed well experientially by my son Chris's comments. After all, I'm not writing this book necessarily for everyone. If you are offended by the title, you'd likely be offended by the book and shouldn't read it. It is targeted for men and hardy female types who can appreciate male humor. The title, and the book as a whole, is also in sync, I think, with the way in which breast cancer has been gradually desexualized and normalized, largely by women, in our culture. Breast cancer was once, like perhaps testicular cancer still is, an uncomfortable, somewhat taboo subject for polite and routine conversation. This is no longer the case. Well done, ladies! Public exposure, even advocacy (note the NFL adopting pink shoes, etc., to highlight public awareness), have brought the subject into the light. Screening, support, and recovery are now much more evident and advanced for breast cancer. Indeed, the normalization has expanded into the adolescent genre (my favorite) with T-shirts and slogans like "We love boobies" and "Save the Tatas." Humor and real life philanthropic endeavors can be combined and done for the common good. I can imagine slogans for testicular cancer might also one day be humorously normalized—i.e., "Go Nads," "Sack Cancer," etc. In any event, the title is too congruent with that mix of humor, adolescence, and reality that the book aims for. I hope you can enjoy and or overcome the title to explore the book and yourself further. As one appreciative reader, Teresa P., said, "You had me at the title," per the movie *Jerry Maguire*.

A Side Note to My Christian Readers:

America has long been considered a death-denying culture. We chase the temporary symbols of youth, sometimes desperately. More is not necessarily better—things or life on earth. Christians can be susceptible to this as well. Belief in *eventual* eternal life in heaven is a promise we hold on to, as we should. But God's timing is not our timing. We too can be prone to deny the reality of our own death because we aspire to be more deeply spiritual and faithful to these promises; the Rapture, the second coming of Christ, will happen—*in our lifetime.* I believe deeply it will happen and eternity is a promise for believers. But the life and death cycle is also God-given. It is His order. As stated in Ecclesiastes 7:2 (NIV), "… For death is the destiny of every man." It behooves us to deal with that order first, knowing that the second coming will happen but not necessarily in our earthly lifetime.

The financial crisis that has hit the world recently can be likened to a cancer—a major illness. It requires a fight, a reordering of life priorities and a clarification of those things most valuable to us. Wealth often gives the illusion of security, control, independence, and freedom—all things that can be significant stumbling blocks to submission, brokenness owned, and a deep spiritual walk. These artifacts of wealth are illusions that we all cling to, Christian and non-Christian alike. They can distort a deeper, higher truth. As the existentialists say, we are thrown into life needing to choose meaning and deal with separation (isolation). We are free to do anything and are responsible for all choices, *and we will die*—the ultimate major calamity but a framework for living authentically. Indeed, from a Christian perspective, "death has been swallowed up in victory." (1 Corinthians 15:55, NIV). Whether it is the reality of personal mortality, a major life-threatening illness, a financial crisis, or a chosen attempt to deal with the God-given order of the life and death cycle, the opportunity to live more deeply, authentically, and in congruence with our chosen values is enriched by a robust response to these realities. You, individually, and

America, as a country, will be enriched in the process—and may God bless your journey in this life and the hereafter.

Romans 5:3–5 (NIV) says, "…And we also rejoice in our suffering, because we know that suffering produces perseverance; perseverance, character; and character, hope. And hope does not disappoint us…" The idea of rejoicing in our suffering is one of the hardest things to wrap our minds around in this life. When we find ourselves in situations that are deemed suffering, we struggle to survive them; finding joy in their midst seems unfathomable. This joy doesn't have the connotation familiar to society, where it is simply a synonym for happiness. It speaks of something deeper, something out of this world, per se. It is an attitude that can be adopted in the midst of anything, that still hopes for something better, believes that this too shall pass, and seeks to find the silver lining. What this scripture talks about is a goal much easier said than done but experientially possible and truly life-changing when accomplished. This book is my attempt at rejoicing in my season of suffering and to empower and inspire you to do the same amidst your sufferings. Joy is simply hope in the darkest of times, and hope cannot be taken away; it cannot disappoint.

This book is dedicated to my wife, Denel, who had to endure the "side-car" status of this whole process. As a friend, Lora W., so aptly put it, "Watching someone die in slow motion is terrible." Denel was my deepest blessing throughout the ordeal. It is also dedicated to all the cancer fighters, no matter what the outcome, and their families and friends whose love and support throughout the ordeal make up the manna we survive on during the trip through the desert of cancer recovery. I especially single out a friend and multiple cancer survivor, Dody J., and her family in this regard. She is the epitome of courage and class, having survived with dignity and grace more episodes of cancer and treatment than can be counted on one hand. She is, as I like to say, the "Babe Ruth" of cancer survival and a model for us all.

Workbook Instructions

This book is written for individuals and groups, in a workbook format, to help confront in a realistic and positive way the realities of personal mortality. It is not about my journey so much as it is about yours. Leaving a legacy to those you love requires some preparation. Everybody is going to die—even you. (Ecclesiastes 7:2 (NIV): "...For death is the destiny of every man; the living should take this to heart.") The question is, "Are you going to live well?" and if so, what does living well mean to you personally? A life well lived is a life well planned. The turmoil, in practical and emotional terms, that ensues from an unplanned death has tremendous consequences to those left behind. I differentiate here between a sudden death and an unplanned death. You can know you are dying for months and years and still not prepare—that is an unplanned death. It is an irresponsible death and can do much to undermine the legacy you hope to leave. Long-term, simmering, emotional conflicts in any family come out in full force over the lack of clarity in your intentions. I have seen it innumerable times in my clinical work as a psychologist in private practice. It is a devastating and unnecessary wound to any family structure.

Even more importantly, perhaps, are the gifts not given—those final words and acts that sum up a life of meaning and purpose in our most cherished relationships. The questions at the end of each chapter can help focus your efforts to bring clarity to these gifts and to how you live. Your family and loved ones, I'm sure, will greatly appreciate your efforts. It may very well change your life by providing clarity to priorities in accord with your deepest desires. This book is thus not for those who want to die but for those who want to live more fully. If depression is part of your life experience prior to or during this process, your participation in the workbook should be screened for readiness and monitored and supported by professional psychotherapy throughout. It is intended to be joyful and meaningful but not lighthearted. I wish you joy, meaning, purpose, and an enriched life in the process.

Self-Test

Answer the following questions *both before and after* going through the book/workbook. It is meant as a self-measure for clarity and can be shared in a group setting or with others if you wish. There are no standards for rightness here. This is a non-standardized assessment tool for self-examination. Hopefully there will be progress from the first to the last administration of the scale. It is up to you to decide how much progress you want. Please circle your response to each question and total the scores at the end.

> 1 = Never, Not at All
> 2 = Very rarely
> 3 = Rarely
> 4 = Sometimes, Partially
> 5 = Often
> 6 = Usually
> 7 = Always, Completely Done

1. I have thought recently and deeply about the legacy I want to leave.

   1   2   3   4   5   6   7

2. I live in accord with my priorities in life.

   1   2   3   4   5   6   7

3. I have reviewed my life and am at peace with my joys and regrets.

   1   2   3   4   5   6   7

4. I have a living will or trust.

   1   2   3   4   5   6   7

5. I have clearly communicated my intentions about cremation/burial and memorial services to my loved ones.

   1   2   3   4   5   6   7

6. I have sufficient life and disability insurance to cover all my financial responsibilities and wishes.

   1   2   3   4   5   6   7

7. I have communicated my deepest feelings to all my loved ones.

     1   2   3   4   5   6   7

8. I am at peace with others.

     1   2   3   4   5   6   7

9. I have DNR (Do Not Resuscitate), power of attorney, and organ donor forms completed and signed.

     1   2   3   4   5   6   7

10. I am at peace with God.

     1   2   3   4   5   6   7

A Word of Caution

Some valuable feedback I got from two friends, Janet and Ms. Mille, who reviewed an early draft of this book, was that the humility and humor of the narrative were engaging and inviting but that then there was the harsh reality of the legacy questions. The flow was from some levity and then to maybe too much depth/reality. It was like *bam!* and very possibly overwhelming for the reader. The transition was too drastic. There is much merit in this feedback. Consequently, I've written a brief introduction to each post-chapter set of legacy questions as an attempt to provide a gentler transition. The legacy workbook is also placed at the end of the manuscript. However, at least two other options might be considered. You can read the whole narrative and then reread it with the legacy questions or simply return to the legacy questions at a later date—your choice. The only potential problem with the last option is that that later date may never happen and denial and avoidance will again rule. In any event, please choose the approach that best fits you and your needs. Authenticity and levity can coexist, as they so often do in real living. The transitional process in this case is yours for the choosing.

THE ROAD
LESS PAVED

"Daddy, can I drive?" It was 1973. My three-year-old daughter, Belinda, and I had just driven our Volkswagen bug into the parking lot of the modular homes at Azusa Pacific College. This housing was reserved for married couples and families. It was still somewhat under construction, so there was a big dirt field next to our modular house. "Sure, honey. Sit on my lap, and I'll help you steer." Belinda gleefully climbed into my lap and grabbed the wheel. She had no clue of the correlation between her movements of the wheel and the movements of the car, but she was powerful and in control, and I guess it is human nature to savor that experience. She quickly turned the wheel hard left. We were headed for that large dirt area with potholes and who knew what else. I was about to "correct" the course when I thought, *Nah, she's having too much fun. Let's just play this out and enjoy the bumpy ride.* It really was quite a ride. We got jostled all around pretty hard, but Belinda's laughter and unabashed joy was well worth any potential damage to the car. Maybe this was a life lesson: enjoying the unpaved road with all the surprises and adventures and trials involved.

Today, in my office, I have a replica Norman Rockwell statue of an adult and two kids headed downhill on a roller coaster. The adult has their eyes covered, and you can sense the fear and trepidation involved in the experience for them. The kids have their eyes wide open and their hands high in the air, enjoying the thrill of the ride. These seem like two microcosms of how we can choose to live life. I have generally had my eyes semi-open, but I am totally white-knuckling my grip on the coaster. Life has been about survival and getting through difficult experiences more than savoring the process like those kids did.

Belinda's mom, Carol, and I had been married in high school. You can guess the circumstances. But I loved her and was willing to fight, struggle, and white-knuckle my way through to make it all work. Carol had other plans and needs. She chose to separate from me later that year. The pain for me with that experience and especially the painful, confused, and innocent eyes of Belinda were truly heartbreaking for me. Despite my efforts to the contrary, Carol and I soon divorced. I had done nothing to "warrant" divorce other than we had just been married too young and Carol wanted to *live*. We were only twenty-one. I can understand now, but I couldn't then. I spent the rest of Belinda's childhood and early adult years trying to pay a debt I never fully owed to her. It was her mom's decision, not mine, but I felt her pain and sometimes got lost in the attempts to alleviate it.

Like so many painful paths, however, there has been much fruit in our relationship. Belinda and I have now come to a peaceful, joyful, and connected relationship without guilt and with much love. I adore her, and she now fully knows and accepts that fact. The process was deeply painful at times for both of us, but God has brought about much healing. The ride has definitely been worth it.

The shame I felt, in addition to the pain from the divorce at a small Christian college in the 1970s, permeated my being for future decades. Although I have participated as a client in much helpful therapy over the years, these issues never fully resolved until quite recently. In the loss of Belinda and the marriage, I had experienced such a drastic change in what I believed defined me. From a young husband and father to a divorced single father at twenty-one was such a painful contrast. In my eyes, I was a failure. I focused on school, surviving, and football, but I was pretty lost. Academically, I did very well. I was desperate because I was, after all, a failure. In fact, I continued to feel like a failure through two master's degrees, three life-teaching credentials, and a PhD. Feelings can often exist despite the facts. Football was a mixed bag. There were some minor triumphs but some very contentious and odd coaching relationships. I did develop some friendships that helped me survive that season of my life and that have challenged me repeatedly since to live more like those kids enjoying the roller coaster. In the end, relationships, not accomplishments, carry the day for us all.

I have three best friends. Bill (Billy), John (Big John), and I have a thirty-five-plus year friendship from our days playing football at Azusa Pacific University. (It was only a college then, APC. They played a lot more than I did.) One of my brothers, Don, is my other best friend. To set the stage, here's some background especially for you football fans about my relationships with Billy and John. Although the level of play at APC then was not nearly as high as it is now, I have a couple of stories about the whole experience that I love to tell. After all, we had the first winning season in the school's history our last year there. Although we were only 5–4, technically we were better than USC—yes, the mighty Trojans of Southern Cal! It goes along with that "on any given Sunday" any team can beat any team (in the NFL). This is the Saturday/college version of that same dynamic. Let me explain. That year (1973), we beat St. Mary's by two points. John, wearing very long, trendy hair at the time, was actually tackled by that hair from behind as it flowed out of the back of his helmet at the one yard line, just short of a touchdown. He took some serious ribbing for that one. To continue my line of shameless reasoning, we beat St. Mary's by two points, St. Mary's beat San Francisco State, San Francisco State beat San Jose State, San Jose State beat Stanford and guess who Stanford beat that year? That's right, USC! Therefore, by my reasoning, we were better than USC in 1973—the same year they were the national champs. In reality, of course, they would have annihilated us, but it's fun to fantasize about and the facts don't lie, but the logic might be faulty, I admit.

Well, I've told this story to anyone who would listen for thirty-five years plus and believed it, wholeheartedly. Unfortunately, in verifying the facts about the scores, teams, and even the year, it turned out to be one of those "stories that grew with the years." From telling to telling, the facts gradually changed and the story grew, even though I was the only one telling it. Somehow the chain of teams wasn't quite right, and I even had the year wrong (it was actually 1972 and 1974 that USC won the national championship, not 1973). As it turns out, San Francisco State did not play San Jose that year, and unlike 1972 and 1974, when USC did win the national championship, I had long immortalized in my own mind, it was actually 1973—a year USC did not win the national championship! I guess, all in all, it was one of those cases where the older I got, the better we used to be. It's a real bummer when reality puts a damper on a good story.

If you are not a football fan and wish to get back to the story, feel free to skip the next football story.

The other story about APC Cougar football I love to tell is when—as a rag-tag, no practice, dressing in uniform scraps at mid-field group of old-aged, out-of shape alumni—we were supposed to be fodder for a Cougar team that had completed two-a-day training. They were in shape and young (some in our group were in their forties by game time). We were supposed to get creamed and forever put to rest any semblance of pride that might have remained from tolerating some exceptionally bad coaching during our time at APC. This alumni game was intended to be a massacre.

The game itself was put together by my buddy Billy. You see, there was a lot of bad blood between the APC head coach at the time, Jerry Sconce, and the veterans on the team. Coach Sconce became head coach my freshman year. He hadn't recruited me (not many of us were actually "recruited"; except for a few, we were just guys who had played high school football, still loved the game, and wanted to keep the dream alive). As a freshman, he might have accepted me as one of his guys (he recruited three players from a small Oregon high school he had coached at), but I was older by two years and, with my high school best friend, Richard, became associated with the older group of "chippers" (people who made negative comments), as Coach Sconce called us. "Chippers" were guys who actually had a brain and could see through the hypocrisy, poor coaching, and lack of capacity to judge talent that Coach Sconce and some of his staff conveyed. From his perspective, we were complainers and nonbelievers in his system. Under his new regime, John went from a pro-prospect quarterback (he lasted eight weeks with the Oakland Raiders training camp after graduation) to a pulling guard for a one-back-carries-all offense. Richard became a blocking back who rarely, if ever, touched the ball. Billy went from an all-league level defensive back and career leader in tackles and interceptions to a blocking tight end before an injury ended his season and career, but it did not end his bitterness toward Coach Sconce.

I was switched to linebacker when all three starting linebackers quit the team in one fell swoop in training camp. I had played quarterback in high school. I didn't think I had a chance at quarterback because John was five inches taller, faster, and threw better than I did. So I tried out for defensive back but made the mistake one day of hitting Richard hard in a drill (he was only going half speed; I thought it was full speed). I looked like a stud for three seconds.

I was one of only two guys on the team who lifted weights (Richard was the other), and I got beat deep too many times at defensive back. So *poof*, I was a linebacker—a 173-pound linebacker! I did have good upper body strength, and I was a ball hawk, so I made some contributions despite my light frame and skinny legs. In fact, I can actually prove it. One day a friend said he had one blurry copy of a copy of a game film from 1973—the Occidental game. Now this was exciting news for me because, short of the alumni game, it was probably my best game in my APC career. I was able to copy the copy of the copy, and I still have it to this day. I look like a quarterback trying to play linebacker. I had this odd, exaggerated stance, but at least in that game I made some big plays. I intercepted two passes (the only two of my career), made the final block on a punt return for a touchdown, and almost made another great play. I say almost because two-thirds of it was picture-perfect. Playing outside backer, a sweep came to my side. I rushed in past the tight end, met the fullback head on, spun around as I put him to the ground, and was set to face the running back yards deep in his own backfield. Now I say two-thirds picture-perfect because it was truly that—perfect to that point. I rushed in, beating any chance for the tight-end to block me—perfect. I met and pushed the blocking fullback to the ground while spinning and readying myself to tackle the running back—perfect.

Now up to that point, it was so picture-perfect that even Coach Sconce could recognize that it was exceptional. In our film session during the week after the game, he ran it over and over again to show how perfectly it was done and how all others should do the same. Of course he asked, "Who is that guy? Number thirty-four?" He had no clue; he often had no clue. But to his credit, he kept showing it up to the square off with the running back because it really was picture-perfect—again, up to that point.

You see, I was a quarterback in a linebacker's uniform. A real linebacker would have relished the opportunity to explode on the running back. Thinking like a quarterback, I just wanted to make sure I got a piece of him and he didn't get away. I knew I'd get help. I'd already beaten two guys, so I was cautious, not attacking, on my heels, and playing it safe like a quarterback, not a linebacker. The running back ran over me; it was ugly. I did get a hold of his shoe and assist in the tackle, but it wasn't pretty. I had that anxiety during the film session where you are the only one that knows the ending and it ain't pretty. Like I said, it was two-thirds perfect. There was a collective "*aah*" from the team when the final part of the play was finally shown in the film session. I went from being a stud to a wuss in the span of a few seconds in the mind of a lot of teammates. Nonetheless, I had a game film to help me remember a few highlights from APC football. I only played two years because of my divorce and my relationship with

Coach Sconce. Our last year together was the first winning season (5–4) for APC football. Coach Sconce was never successful to any significant degree at APC, although subsequent coaches were.

Anyway, back to the alumni game. The bad blood between Coach Sconce and us now-recent grads was thick in the air. When Billy got this crazy idea to play an alumni game, Coach Sconce jumped at the chance. In one fell swoop, he would put to rest many "chippers" who questioned his wisdom. After all, the deck was clearly stacked. We would have a hard time even fielding a complete team—few of us would be in shape, none of us would be in football shape, and we wouldn't have practiced even once before game time! What's more, Coach Sconce scheduled the game for the end of two-a-day fall football practice immediately preceding a new season of Cougar football. His team would be primed and ready. Billy either was delusional or a true visionary. There should have been no way we could have even stayed on the field with those guys. He had way more confidence than we had in ourselves or than anyone in their right mind should've had.

Once game day was upon us, we realized we had no equipment. We were given extra pieces of uniforms, scraps, leftovers, castoffs, and any other reject term you can think of from the team. It was the thrift store version of uniform equipment. And frankly, it matched the caliber of our team that day. We gathered at midfield and went through the junk we were given. Suited in our piecemeal uniforms, together we turned in unison and saw, to our horror, eighty current Cougar football team members fully practiced and in tip-top shape, lined up like an army (in new uniforms to boot), heading onto the field. *Oh my*, I thought. *We're going to get creamed!* Needless to say, Coach Sconce had us right where he wanted us. The one concession granted to us was that there would be simplified special teams play, specifically no kick-offs. Each team just took possession of the ball at their own thirty yard line.

We were truly a motley crew. I was in good shape. I worked out and ran, but not for football. Billy and his brother Bob weren't in great shape, but they were natural athletes and able to compete on a Saturday morning after too much "Friday night," if necessary. John was as talented as ever but clearly out of shape. Richard and Bill McCorkle were probably the most ready to play; they were always mentally and somewhat physically in football shape, although they hadn't played in several years. Bill also had his previous experience as a Little All-American on his side. Otherwise, we were ugly—I mean ugly out of shape, out of tune, out of touch, out of our minds. Tom Nelson, forty-plus years old at the time, a former player and coach, insisted on playing and quarterback at that! He moved so slowly, and he got hit so hard one time his glasses were all tweaked. He retired permanently after that play—smart move, Tom.

I was to play defensive end. Why? I don't know; I'd never played there before, and nobody else wanted it. I guess it was like one of those volunteer situations where I didn't step forward but everyone else stepped backward faster or just laid dibs to other positions. Really, we were making it up as we went. So the first series we were on defense. I remembered the famous head slap and swim move David Deacon Jones somewhat immortalized with the LA Rams in the 1960s (it's illegal now). I used it often, and to my great surprise, it worked very well. The first drive we were doing okay, but they were gradually moving the ball. Bill McCorkle called for a stunt with me and the tackle next to me, Ernie Chapin. Ernie had played defensive line his entire career, but I'd never been there. I understood my job on the stunt was to slant inside across the tackle and take him into the guard over Ernie. Ernie would pause and then slant off my rear toward my position. The idea was to confuse the blocking scheme and free Ernie up to make the tackle. It worked to perfection. I took my tackle into the guard, and they were both tangled up, blocking me. Ernie was now free, unblocked, just as planned. The running back coincidentally went right into the hole Ernie had slanted into—or so we thought. We had the perfect play called, but the running back got a long gainer and they eventually scored a touchdown.

When we asked Ernie what happened, he said it had been so long since he played that he just kept running past the area he was supposed to occupy. He ended up near the sidelines, I think in a somewhat confused state. Oh yeah, we were rusty. As we were coming off the field after their touchdown, Richard asked me what happened, thinking I'd gotten beaten. You wouldn't believe it, Rich!

We settled down after that. We shut them down completely. They never scored again. I had arguably my best game ever. I was beating the person blocking me so regularly that they switched the tackle three times and the tight end two times to try to stop me. I was putting pressure on the quarterback, and Coach Sconce couldn't believe how a "little rat" could do that. That is what he called all those who didn't think like him. Insult, not to be confused as affection. There was no love lost either way. He even tried a screen pass to the tight end to slow me down. I read that too and tackled him for a two-yard loss. Eventually he just gave up, I guess, and double-teamed me by keeping a back in to help block for the entire fourth quarter. The fact that the back would sometimes go for my knees was not appreciated and I told him so, in a not-too-friendly manner.

Near the end of the game, we hadn't scored, and they were ahead 6–0. John, rolling out on one play, gradually had his out-of-shape legs give out on him. It was hilarious to see. It looked like he was running slowly down an escalator as he ran himself into the ground, untouched by any tackler. It didn't look like we would score. So we put a punt block on. It worked. I escorted the player who picked up the ball into the end zone. We made the extra point and were ahead 7–6! Now with our defense in control, we could actually do the impossible and win the game! We did our job and shut their offense down for the last time. We got the ball. All we had to do was run out the clock, and we would win the game. John asked Bob if he could beat their defensive back deep. Bob always thought he could beat everybody deep, so he of course said, "Yeah!" John was putting the game at risk if there was a turnover, but whatever—a touchdown would be extra sweet. We all wanted, needed, something special out of this game. He threw his best pass of the day, and Bob caught it in the end zone. Alumni win 13–6!

We were ecstatic. We shook the hands of the players on the other team and sincerely wished them well for the season. After all, we were all still Cougars. They were in shock. Coach Sconce was humiliated, fuming, and less than gracious. As was typical of his style, he was so angry with his team for losing that he made them run wind sprints on the field after the game. This was a shaming experience for them and disgusting to us. No matter how old, out of shape, and ill-prepared we were, we were still ballplayers. We beat them. They didn't lose. He didn't understand a lot about football or people or character.

A lesson for me in shame followed. After the game, the excitement lingered. It felt like we'd done the impossible and righted so many wrongs at the same time. Unfortunately, even several years later at this alumni game, and despite my success in the game, I had a hard time staying on the field and soaking it in. It was a time for celebration, but I hadn't yet learned to do that very well. I still carried shame with me—deep shame. I just couldn't stay there. I was still carrying too many painful, shameful memories. So I left the field and met up with the guys later to celebrate. I then found out that my inner circle of friends had taken a picture together on the field after I'd left. I was heartbroken but learned a lesson that day. It is okay to let shame go, to celebrate and enjoy, to relish overcoming—not overcoming others, but myself. It was my shame, not their perception of me, that held me back. I got a copy of that picture and taped a picture of myself in the group as a reminder to never let shame hold me back again. I cherish that picture to this day. It is above my desk at home.

BALANCING OPPOSITES

This book, as I've said, is not about Jerry. I just wanted you as the reader to understand enough about me to get a feel for the canvas on which God eventually painted a beautiful picture through the love and prayers of other people. Through this experience, I was given the rare opportunity to essentially be present at my own funeral and to see how deeply others cared for me. My life had been meaningful. This was, in my mind, despite all that I had or had not "accomplished" in my life, a true measure of a life well lived. Other people knew how much I loved them and wanted to give back. Like George in the movie *It's a Wonderful Life*, getting to experience the love that was given to me, at least in part in response to the love I'd given, was my little miracle.

To summarize, then, who I am, who I was, the canvas on which God painted this picture: highly accomplished (= insecure); unique thought process (= weird); very loving (= heartfelt intentions, often misguided); well-rounded individual after the ancient Greek model of mind/body balance (= not *really* good at anything); always trying to do the right thing (= why try?; every time I go over the lines I get nailed); highly intelligent (= I like to pretend I'm smart; sometimes I fool people); well educated (= I do persevere; as my buddy John says, I have more degrees than Carter has pills); well-read (= trying, I am on #67 of the world's greatest books, but does it really matter if, as my brother Don says, I have a memory like Swiss cheese?); humble (= I know *all* the dirt on me; if anyone should be humble, it is I); favorite philosopher, Socrates (= know thy self; the Oracle of Delphi essentially said his wisdom came from his acknowledgement that he knew nothing! = I am constantly running into my limitations); self-deprecating (= if the shoe fits, etc.); a Myers-Briggs INFJ (= an introverted, intuitive, feeling, and closure-oriented dude). I double-majored in philosophy and physical education at APC because I didn't know what I wanted to do (or who I was!) and I figured that anything I did after that career-wise would have to fall between those two extremes. In short, I am a combination of my mother (intellectual, artist) and my father (hard worker, mechanic).

This book will hopefully become about you, not me. I hope it becomes a tool to refine, sharpen, and enhance the legacy you want your life to be. As with most of us, we try to plan the particulars of our lives, we try to pave the road ahead. Inevitably, the life we actually live will be on the unpaved road. I wish you much enjoyment on the ride and fruit for yourself and others.

After I got accepted to attend USC for my PhD program, a friend remarked what a great accomplishment that was and expressed surprise that I wasn't more excited. I told him that I felt that what other people decided (acceptance or not) didn't define me and therefore this wasn't much of an accomplishment. But what was an accomplishment, what I was proud of, I readily shared with him. As a then-teacher at Lanterman State Hospital for the Developmentally Disabled, I had in my team-taught class (a shout out to Gary, Carol, Marty, and Donna!) a group of students with multiple disabilities (mental functioning and mobility/motor functioning). One particular student, named "Elizabeth," was very resistant, strong, and strong-willed about one part of our curriculum-ambulation. She preferred her wheelchair, even though she was capable of walking. We had measured and marked the entire route to our classroom from the resident living cottages and developed individual goals for each of our students related to progress in ambulation along this path. Elizabeth was a large girl, mid to late teens, and was very strong-bent against any walking, as I've said. She was just fine in that wheelchair from her perspective. However, I was just as pig-headed as her. I guess we were a lot alike. In any event, we were clearly pitted against each other in this process. One day I went into the cottage and, walking up behind her wheelchair as she was facing away from me, I informed her that it was time for class. She knew what that meant and would have no part of it. She quickly reached back over her shoulder in an attempt to scratch/poke/generally protest her predicament. Her fingers had nails that apparently hadn't been clipped in a while, so they were essentially five little weapons at her disposal. She caught me just under my right eye, skipped over the eye, and caught me again above the same eye. I was bleeding, not badly, but very stunned. I was very fortunate that I still had my right eye. But in that environment with so many germs and possible infections, any wound meant two hepatitis shots for me as a precaution. I guess you could say Elizabeth was, at least at this time and for me, a pain in the butt. Well, two actually (pun intended).

Despite losing that battle, I didn't give up. I generally don't. This is sometimes a strength and sometimes a weakness in me. Eventually Elizabeth realized this and seemed to understand that my intentions were good. We began to build a bond. After a while, she would actually light up when I came into her unit. The days of attacking me were clearly over. Her mobility greatly improved. In relaying this story to my friend, I told him that, from my perspective, at both a relationship and educational/growth level, this was a real accomplishment, not whether USC said I could join their club or not. I had learned that lesson a few years before when UCLA had declined my application to their master's degree program in special education. My goals in that area and their program focus were not a good match, and I know that objectively now, but when it happened I internalized it, lumped it together with every other self-perceived failure, and was crushed. Yes, I cried (like a ninnybaby!). As an aside, this whole USC/UCLA section is a thinly disguised attempt to get all Trojan/ Bruin lovers into dispute (kind of like what Paul did with the Pharisees and the Sanhedrin over resurrection). To further complicate and enmesh my readers in debate, I was and still am a Bruin (UCLA) and Notre Dame fan and not a USC fan (despite the best efforts of my wife and my friend Ken, both true Trojans and alumni, to convert me).

Years later, I ran into Elizabeth in the community at a hamburger stand. She was with a group of other former Lanterman Hospital clients now living in a group home in the community. She didn't fully recognize me, but there was a glimmer in her eyes like she saw someone she knew. What she gave me and, hopefully, what I gave her, even for a season, was a real accomplishment. Two people had touched each other to the betterment of both. I will always remember her. What we can control defines us far more than what we can't. As it says in Galatians 5:6 (NIV), "…The only thing that counts is faith expressing itself through love."

DIAGNOSIS: A LIFE SHATTERED

One can hardly imagine just how fragile life is until they experience the lightning-fast way in which it changes in the time it takes for one heart to beat, one sentence to be spoken, one phone to ring. Sometimes it seems like our lives are just a ticking time bomb until we get one of those calls. At least that's how it seemed for me.

I have always worked very hard, been very healthy, and had tons of energy. My buddy Billy says, "I've got guilt and shame issues, so I've got to work harder than anybody else on the planet." If you add a deep sense of inadequacy, that pretty well describes me. Although my life has been very hard because of how these issues have affected it, I have been blessed. I worked out and ran very regularly. For a little old guy, I was pretty strong. A few years ago I had my first health problem, some weird thing called celiac disease. It is essentially an allergy to the protein gluten, which is in every good-tasting bread and pastry item in the world! Imagine a Frenchman who loves bread and suddenly couldn't eat any. The alternatives are flours called quinoa, soy, rice, potato starch, sorghum, garbanzo/fava bean, Indian ricegrass, etc., most of which your dog wouldn't eat. Eventually I was able to find a few staples I could eat (I buy my gluten-free pretzels by the case), grieved my roots, and adjusted. It really is a serious illness, and the average elapsed time to diagnosis in the United States is nine years. It is a genetic predisposition in some people of Northern European descent. It is diagnosed much quicker in Europe. There has apparently been some resistance by the American medical community to recognize the disease for some reason. I was very fortunate that my Kaiser doctors were able to diagnose it in short order. It is totally controlled with the right diet (if that doesn't kill you!). Consequently, my health returned, and so did my energy. I carried on with my usual work and activity pattern. I was even able to find more and more foods and even a few restaurants that had a clue what I was talking about when I asked about gluten-free menu items. Life, as I knew it, returned to normal—at least as normal as it can be for a psychologist in private practice.

I was never that good in football, but I made two lifetime friendships that are priceless. A bond that started through football has continued and grown through nearly four decades. From sharing football, Billy, John, and I now share all of life together.

The three of us had just gotten together at Priest Lake in Idaho. We have an endless series of jokes aimed distinctly at Billy (forehead—ever expanding, airplane landing strip, etc.), John (nose—ginormous), and me (racial heritage) that we never seem to tire of. Of course, I always win in these playful put-down contests. After all, it's my book; do you think I'd say I lost? We are genuinely connected and cherish the time together. We laugh a lot. It is a wonderful medicine. We aren't nearly as active as in our younger years, what with their man-boobs and my skinny legs and inability to tolerate the cold. On this trip, we mostly just talked, ate, rode around in the boat, and drank huckleberry margaritas. We had our usual great time. I was in the lake twice for about thirty seconds each time: once on the spur of the moment, and once to tie up the boat near shore.

However, when I got home, I started having some intestinal problems. It got bad enough where I was losing sleep. From all indications, it appeared to be an exacerbation of the celiac disease. Although it is controlled by a gluten-free diet, that was harder to accomplish than I realized at the time. There are wheat/bread products often used in sauces and other items that you wouldn't suspect. Since the effects of gluten are cumulative, the symptoms happen after—sometimes significantly after—exposure.

I tightened up my diet further and went to see my gastroenterologist, Dr. Marnoy. He scheduled a CT scan, but within a few days, my symptoms disappeared, and I was feeling fine (also with the help of an antibiotic—I had picked up a parasite from the lake). We agreed to cancel the CT scan. He called me the next day and suggested, on second thought, that it might be a good idea to go ahead with the scan and that we could use it as a baseline for future monitoring of the celiac. Maybe this was godly intervention. I agreed and had the scan.

What followed shortly thereafter was a somewhat alarming amount of attention from several doctors. I was the focus of attention in a way that made me kind of nervous. As I soon discovered, the CT scan had detected a tumor in my abdomen. Together with the parasite and the celiac activity, I was more of a mess than I realized. The tumor was the scary thing, though. The doctor then scheduled me for a needle biopsy. The very sound of that was a bit ominous if all the rest wasn't already too much to bear.

My wife, Denel, and I were stunned. The biopsy was scheduled for a day she worked, and frankly, if I could shield her from some of the road that appeared ahead of me, that was desirable. My brother Don—whom I call the "Duke of Big" because he is royal and large in character to me—was more than willing to go with me for the biopsy. If things looked really bad, he was one of a few people that I would want to entrust the eventual care of my family and disposition of my will/intentions to. He is a rock and a very good man. Being a Vietnam veteran, he should be studied by the VA for a paradigm of hardiness and perseverance despite exposure to the chaos and trauma of that war. He is a pillar of strength. I needed him. I was scared, but I also had a strange peace forming.

The doctor who performed the biopsy was gentle, respectful, and caring. The procedure was pretty strange. They used a CT scan to target a tube insert in my back. They numbed the area and went in an inch at a time with repeat scans to remain precisely on target. After the tube was inserted all the way, they put a needle in the tube and took snips repeatedly—it was relatively tolerable pain-wise but an exhausting emotional process. After the procedure, the doctor was notably kinder and gentler with me. Although this was appreciated, it left me thinking I was in even more serious trouble. Don and I went out to a late breakfast. I gave him some of my preliminary thoughts about what I wanted and needed him to do if I died. He reassured me but also noted the extra step-up in kindness by the doctor after the procedure.

It wasn't long before we got the news. I had stage 2 or 3 testicular cancer. The stages have to do with metastasis—how far it has spread in the body. Stage 1 means it is localized to a testicle with a very high cure rate. Indeed, testicular cancer is one of the most curable of cancers. Stage 2 means it has spread to the lymph nodes in the abdominal area. Stage 3, the highest stage, means it has spread to the chest and/or other areas as well. Testicular cancer is generally a young man's disease. I guess I could take some solace in that an old guy got it, but I have never been typical; unique, odd, different, special, weird—all apply. I had cancer. Cancer. The "C" word. If it hadn't been for the celiac and the parasite, I wouldn't have been diagnosed. I essentially had no symptoms for a cancer that had been in my body for likely several years. What do we do now?

I was fifty-seven years old when I was diagnosed with the cancer. 1 had three children, mostly grown (thirty-eight, twenty-two, and eighteen); two young-adult adopted children; and four grandchildren. I had lived life—a hard life—in the manner I wanted to. I was a giver, a responsible man, and a professional. Far from perfect, but I had lived life as well as I thought I could—it was meaningful. I had loved many personally and helped many professionally. If I had it to do over, I don't think I could do significantly better—unless, of course, God told me to do it significantly differently. I was (and am) a Christian with a peace about the afterlife. I was resolved from the beginning to do everything I could to live but without a need to control the outcome.

As it states in 1 Corinthians 15:26: "…The last enemy to be destroyed is death." We Christians believe death is destroyed with eternal salvation from Jesus Christ. Death is also destroyed when it is faced and facilitates our living well by prioritizing what we most value, knowing there is a last chapter for us all. My need was to plan for it and to do that without denial while ensuring that those I loved knew it and were taken care of.

But there were other needs than mine. Denel, my bride of twenty-three years, had been married before to a police officer killed in the line of duty (Ken Wrede, West Covina PD). She had been married eleven months at the time. Meeting her after that tragedy, I knew full well the pain of that recovery. It took years, and I'm not sure it can ever be totally done. But the cruelty of the possibility that Denel would be burying her second husband was deeply painful to me. In addition, Belinda, my thirty-eight-year-old daughter, had lost her mother to cancer a couple of years earlier.

Jerry Duprez

At any age, being an orphan is a unique and painful experience. If that weren't enough, our neighbor friend, Armando, had died when his two children, Gabe and Angel, were very young. Although I had never formally adopted them, I had done what I could to act like a dad for them. It was always second best but hopefully helpful to them. The thought that they would be burying their second dad, Denel her second husband, and of Belinda being an orphan, together with missing my youngest daughter Nicole's wedding, it seemed like God was cruel or asleep to allow this calamity.

I'm not special. I'm going to die just like everybody else. But this pain seemed too much. I would wake up at night, cry, and write my good-byes, trying to understand. Eventually, I got a peace. Yes, these were sad, even tragic, things if I did die, but Denel and I had had nearly a quarter century together. She knows how much I love her. We've both been blessed by our time together, even if it has to end. I would have some time—sweet and special time—with Belinda. Even if the worst case scenario played out, it would afford us that time unique to humans when all else fades away but the relationship and cherishing each other. Gabe and Angel, as young adults, know that they've been loved by two dads: the best one, Armando, and a decent pinch hitter, me. What I had given them was not diminished by what was to potentially come; it was still all worth it. We were all blessed.

The four years leading up to the diagnosis of my cancer were the worst years of my life. We bought a small office building to house our practice. Despite having several pastors and many friends pray over the site and the building, everything that could go wrong did go wrong many times over. One friend, John S., even asked if we had inadvertently built the building on an old Indian burial ground. The air conditioning went out nearly a dozen times, often in one-hundred-plus-degree heat. We eventually discovered that the original contractor had apparently hooked up one of the two air conditioners in reverse. The plumbing backed up nearly as often as the air conditioning malfunctioned. Each time, rooter drain cleaning gave us the false hope that the problem was fixed, but we would later find our organic friends resurfacing. We eventually found out that the original plumbing contractor had a three-inch elbow pipe fall into a four-inch straight pipe while it was still on his truck en route to the building site. He installed the section of pipe without knowing this. It worked for brief periods of time until it, once again, would clog because of the narrowed opening in the pipe. The contractor, having located the exact problem section of the pipe with a camera, was quite confident that he had chewed it up and, as he put it, "sent it to the ocean."

Another plumber, who I had much more trust in, simply said, "No way. The only way to get that elbow out is to jack-hammer the floor, dig up the ground, and cut the pipe out"—a major project and mess. We went ahead with this plan with apologies to all the women who wanted to use the now-demolished bathroom. After they got down to the pipe and cut it out, he found the culprit. The elbow was clearly chewed on but still lodged tightly in its original bend in the drain pipe. They were able to retrieve the elbow and replace the section of pipe. I had the elbow mounted on a small trophy stand with the inscription "James 1:2, 'Consider it pure joy, my brothers, whenever we face trials of many kinds because you know that the testing of your faith develops perseverance,'" together with, "Romans 5:4–5: '...And perseverance character, and character hope and hope does not disappoint us.'" I felt tested, bombarded, and beaten. I didn't feel any joy about this whole process, but at least we had some positive, painful, and expensive closure. I needed to frame some of this in a positive light. Given the four years of family tragedies, struggles, the building stressors and fiascos, and working myself nearly to death in the process, this truly was the worst four years of my life and possibly the most refining for changing me. A friend, Robin, put it best when she told my wife, "Jerry getting cancer is like the cherry on top of a poop Sunday." Yes, indeed, but maybe fertilizer for growth as well. We were beaten down to the very point of deeply questioning our faith. It all seemed way too much *before* the cancer.

I had been down before (haven't we all). I had gone through a divorce while at APC. It was a crushing, brokenhearted experience and, given the environment, shameful as well. I can still remember my brother Mike coming to rescue me in that pain. The vision of him driving up in the parking lot at APC in his Karmen Ghia is still very clear to me. Love is expressed in many different ways—that is a picture in my mind of love that I will always cherish.

My last year and a half at APC was an experience, to say the least. I was able to stay with a friend, Richard, in his dorm because, as a resident assistant, he had a spare bed. I had no key and needed to use a plastic card to force the lock open each time I wanted to get in. It was much appreciated from Rich ("Beauregard" I called him, from our high school French class days), but it was an empty, odd feeling. I felt like I didn't really belong anywhere, and I was deeply pained by the loss of time with my daughter Belinda and the loss of the marriage. I felt like a phantom—an odd combination of empty, loss, and pain.

I then had to live in my van for my last year of school because Rich had graduated. (Miracle of miracles, huh, Beauregard?) I would park behind the men's dorm and sleep. The van had no dashboard insulation. Winter months were painfully cold, but the other months were tolerable. My friends would periodically come by and rock the van to disturb, harass, and play with me. I would get up before five in the morning, sneak in the dorm, take a shower, and go to work at Lanterman State Hospital by six. I worked as an instructional aide with developmentally delayed clients. School officials eventually became aware of my condition. I was even spoken of with great empathy during one chapel service but was never addressed directly. I appreciated the freedom and felt cared about in the *laissez-faire* approach.

Although it was a very hard time because I was truly down, nearly out, and very broken, it was also a very rich and positive time for me. Almost everything that was meaningful in my life had been stripped away, but

Jerry Duprez

despite it being a crawl, I could still move forward. I grew a lot in self-reliance and demystifying struggles. There could still be hope in the midst of abject despair. I really could see a lot of good coming from such a broken place. Maybe it was training for the cancer recovery later.

My parents gave me twenty-five dollars a week to eat/live on during the week. It wasn't a lot, but I could get two meals a day out of it. I lost five pounds every week and then went home after working the Friday night shift of my second job. My mom would feed me well over the weekend. I would regain the weight and head off to school on Monday morning for another week. My dad would work on my rickety van every weekend to get it to last me another week. My folks were definitely there in my valley with me. I felt great a year after graduating when I was able to give my parents the money back they had given me to eat on. They didn't expect it back, but it felt great to give back. Giving back is, I believe, healing and enriching. It makes the giver a better person. I had already paid them $500 when I realized I could refinance my car and pay them the other $1,000—not in dribs and drabs, but in a lump sum. I had checks made out to each for $500 so they could do what they each wanted to do separately. They both cried—a beautiful gift repaid.

I remember one night in particular where it did get to me, though, where it all felt like too much for me to bear. I was driving home to my parents' house in Gardena late on a Friday night. My gas gauge didn't work well, so I sometimes had to operate in the blind with it. I ran out of gas on the 91 Freeway in Cerritos, still about fifteen miles from home. I was truly penniless. It wasn't just misjudgment. I had nothing left from the week. I raged on my dilapidated dashboard with a lot of pent-up anger at my plight. I had *no* resources, *no* way out of this mess. I was done for, empty (gas tank and me), alone, and defeated. After raging and beating up my dashboard, I sat in bewilderment. I felt so alone. I turned everything off in my brain and sat in the dark on the side of the freeway. Then I thought maybe I had some change in my glove box. Given my financial condition, I was sure it wouldn't be much, if anything, but to my surprise, some hope was kindled as I found thirty-nine cents, all pennies. This is not a lot of money, even in the 1970s, but I chose a direction and headed out on foot in hopes of finding a gas station. I had only faint hopes that thirty-nine cents would buy me any or enough gas to get home, but it was my only option at the time. I found a gas station about a mile away. It was around midnight, but, praise God, it was still open. The guy looked at me like "Are you kidding?" but graciously gave me some gas in a can and accepted my wallet for collateral that I would return the can. I walked back, put the gas in, primed the engine, and got the old van started. I returned the can and headed for home, hoping to get within walking distance and fix it all the next day with my dad. Well, another blessing, I don't know how, but I made it all the way home. My dad gave me a gas credit card, to be used only in emergencies, for the future. I never used it but was extremely grateful for the peace of mind and what God can do with thirty-nine cents!

As I mentioned earlier, my divorce set me apart from the community at APC. There was not then, and I'm not sure if there is now, a context for Christians to understand and deal with divorce. It seemed to represent such failure and shame. In addition to the pain, it put a blackness into the valley I was already enduring. It wasn't that I was judged exactly, although I'm sure I was by some; it was that there was no real community of understanding on campus. It just didn't happen. The support I occasionally received was only from a place of mystification and confusion. They didn't know how to support me, but the efforts, when recognized, were much appreciated.

Cliff Hamlow was the head basketball coach at APC at the time. He had won so many games during his career that he was called the John Wooden of small college sports. Although we had no direct relationship, what was best about a small private school was very much present at APC. I was known and cared about, even if from afar. The only real dealing we had had was on the football field very briefly. He had been notified of my physical exam results and wanted to talk/show support. Despite being in excellent physical shape, my blood pressure was very high—160/100 high. He asked if there was anything troubling me. I couldn't tell him that my wife and I had already decided to separate and that I was stressed and brokenhearted. He later came to understand this after we separated and after the season had ended. I could tell he was awkward as he playfully approached me. He was trying to check in and show support. I felt very cared about. It was much appreciated. When I called him to thank him twenty-five years later, he had no clue what event I was talking about. But it made a difference to me. During a very dark time in my life, someone reached out to me. It was awkward but even more appreciated because I know he had no idea how to help. The caring was in the attempt. The substance of caring was conveyed regardless of form. I think that needs to be remembered when you "don't know how to help" others in strange situations. The attempt is a loving act if done with a sincere heart.

This whole period in my life—the four years leading up to the diagnosis of cancer—was a huge challenge to my faith. I felt at the time that I had sought God's direction more than ever before and frankly felt horribly let down by Him. What I eventually came to understand, at least with the building issue, was that it really was *my* plan with a lot of camouflaged effort by me to get God to cosign it. I've given this to God now—or at least I'm actively trying to—and will let Him redeem it all. I am just not gifted in discerning the will of God very well—there's just too much Jerry in the way. I will keep trying to get out of His way.

THE TOWER OF BABEL

With the diagnosis of testicular cancer, it was time to see the urologist/surgeon. For you nonmedical folks out there, that's big talk for the wiener doctor who was going to cut me quite possibly in places I only want gently and passionately touched by my loving wife. Not a pretty picture.

The day came fairly quickly for the appointment. We were led into a waiting room and sat down. We hadn't been given or hadn't noticed the doctor's name at that point. After we looked over and saw his name, we both started laughing—Dr. Wang! My urologist was named Doctor Wang. We were giggling like two school kids in class. That's not all; we then noticed that his first name was Yu. We lost it at that point. My urologist/surgeon's name was Dr. Yu Wang! Now as it turns out, he was a fantastic doctor—compassionate, honest, and skilled. He probably had more to do with my eventual survival than anyone, but we were giggling when he entered the room. He probably thought we were nuts. Why not Dr. Peter Penis or Dr. Stanley Scrotum? This was all too surreal and funny, but that wasn't the end. As it turned out, Dr. Wang's physician's assistant, a very kind and compassionate clinician himself, carried the name "Mr. Babcock." This is all true; I couldn't make it up.

Denel, being a social worker and problem solver, was equipped with pen and pad to ask questions and record answers with Dr. Wang (he pronounces it Wong; I think you can guess why). Dr. Wang was gracious and let us ask questions but didn't pull any punches either. Denel was determined to clarify the stage of the cancer. I already knew it was stage 2 or 3 and frankly didn't understand why that was hard for her to grasp.

It got worse. Dr. Wang proceeded to describe the largest tumor in the abdomen as *massive*. He used that precise word three times, and Denel somehow didn't hear either it or the word *tumor*. Later she was still trying to sort out stage 1 or 2 and the "enlarged lymph node" that she did hear. God blessed us at that point. I knew He was in charge. For Denel to be confused at that point is atypical to who she is. She was trying to sort out stage 1 or 2 with an enlarged lymph node when it was clear I was at stage 3—the highest stage with testicular cancer—with an inoperable tumor, seventeen centimeters in size. I wasn't even stage 3; in my mind, I was Stage Toast.

It was during the appointment that I again felt the hand of God in the whole process. The first time was the strange peace and courage I felt with the needle biopsy, which is not like me—I'm usually a wimp with pain. When I say I felt God's control at that time, I don't mean that I knew I was going to live. But I knew God was operating and in charge. For Denel to be so off at that time was a true blessing. It was a godly confusion that let her accept the reality of the situation gradually in a way that was not overwhelming to her. God was gently easing her out of her denial at a pace that she could handle. It underscored the psalmist in Psalm 23:4 (NIV): "Even though I walk through the valley of the shadow of death, I will fear no evil, for you are with me." I was definitely in the shadow of death. Would that be the end result? I didn't know, but I now knew I was not alone. Thank you, Lord.

With the modern technological marvels of today, Dr. Wang was able to show us, on the computer in the room, pictures of the tumor. I said it just looked black/gray with a little outer edge of a different color. It made no sense to me. He said that little edge is the only part of my vital organs not covered by the tumor. He said he had not seen this type of cancerous tumor that large or that high in the body, ever.

The cancer went significantly high up into my body, engulfing my vital organs. In addition, the tumor had enmeshed itself in the main intersection of veins and arteries, words my knowledge of anatomy only remotely understood: vena cava, aorta, etc. What was clear was that this area was too vital and sensitive to operate on. Dr. Wang said he couldn't operate, even if he wanted to. The largest tumor was too large, and with one slip of the scalpel, I would lose my life or a vital organ in the higher area. Not a pretty picture—close to hopeless.

The usual procedure with testicular cancer was to remove the involved testicle—the original site of the cancer—and then proceed with chemotherapy.

Additional surgery needs would then be determined by the impact of the chemotherapy. However, because the major tumor (there were also spots in the chest cavity) was so "massive," Dr. Wang recommended we start with chemotherapy first. He said we could take the testicle out anytime—pretty cavalier with my nard but the least of my concerns at that point.

Cancer of any sort is a pretty personal experience, but testicular cancer was, at least for me, especially personal. These are my nards we're talking about here. It was less revealing to tell people I had cancer than to specify that I had testicular cancer. Yeah, my nards have malfunctioned—any surprise?

The first appointment with Dr. Wang also involved the first of what turned out to be many indignities of this type of cancer. Dr. Wang, in front of my wife, was examining my "area." He said, "Well, it's smaller," and then paused for what seemed like an eternity to me. Now no guy wants a doctor (or anybody) to use the term "smaller" when describing his "area." The pause and the effect it had on me in front of my wife (who knows full well my limitations but is gracious enough not to speak out loud about them) was an indignity that proved to be the first of many. Finally, Dr. Wang finished his sentence, "Well, it's smaller...than the other one." Thanks doc; you left me hanging there way too long. At least now we had a direction. It was off to the oncology department for chemotherapy.

CHEMOTHERAPY: THE WONDERFUL HORROR

Everyone has probably heard stories about the ravages of chemotherapy. It is devastating to the human body, but it is also a powerful healing agent in the recovery process from serious cancerous tumors. It saved my life, I'm sure. There were times throughout chemo that living seemed undesirable, which gives some insight into the intensity of taking intravenous poisons into your system.

I am a highly educated Christian. My education gives me a vocabulary sufficient to describe most anything with non-offensive words. My spiritual beliefs lead me toward moral positions averse to cussing. However, there is one swear word that, simply put, best describes the experience of chemotherapy. I apologize in advance if this is offensive to you. You are welcome to skip this chapter if you wish because I will use this one cuss word repeatedly. It best reflects the guttural depth of the experience of chemotherapy.

Chemotherapy has made significant progress in the past decade or so in refining dosages, drugs, and types of cancer. It is much more targeted than in the past but still has a long way to go. Indeed, if oncologists (poison doctors) are fully honest, they would say that chemotherapy is the "'kill shit' philosophy of medicine." Although the chemo drugs are specific and somewhat targeted, they kill without regard. They kill good and bad cells in the body without a truly focused, selective plan. There is no engineer running the train once the drugs are in your system. An honest but hypothetical conversation with a chemo nurse or oncologist would go like this:

Jerry: So these powerful drugs you are giving me are going to kill the cancer?

Nurse/Oncologist: Oh yeah. They will kill lots of stuff.

Jerry: You mean they will kill the cancer, right?

Nurse/Oncologist: Well, yeah, that's what we hope.

Jerry: You mean it may not kill the cancer?

Nurse/Oncologist: Well, we know it will kill shit in your body—bad shit, good shit. It will definitely kill shit.

Jerry: I don't understand. It will kill bad shit or good shit?

Nurse/Oncologist: Trust me; this shit is poison, and it will kill shit—lots of shit—bad shit *and* good shit. It is the state of the art, and let's just say it's a fairly new art.

You can see from this hypothetical conversation where I get the label the "'kill shit' philosophy of medicine." My oncologist, Dr. Shu (shoo the cancer away?), put it in similar terms. He said the goal is to "take you to the brink of death and then bring you back." I guess this is the best way to maximize the "kill shit" component in the whole process.

Again, part of the surreal quality to the whole experience is that although I probably had this cancer in my body for a number of years, I had no symptoms. *No* pain, *no* symptoms. Working out, running, and work were in full gear up to the start of chemotherapy. We kept waiting to wake up from the nightmare. I was immediately started on a chemotherapy regimen that included three poisons… er, drugs. These were Cisplatin, Etoposide, and Bleomycin. Now to help you understand these drugs and their impact on the human body, I give you their Latin origin ("Jerry Latin," that is) and a pronunciation guide as follows:

Cisplatoshit   Sis-plato-shit
Etoposhit   E-topo-shit
Bleoh my this is bad shit
Ble-oh-my-this-is-bad-shit

As you can see, the root words are all similar. The nurses even have a phrase that is consistent with this terminology: they will "flush" you with saline solution at times. As you can see, my framing of the whole experience is not far off the mark. Indeed, the Bleomycin is so toxic that *for the rest of my life* if I ever need surgery with a general anesthetic, I am supposed to let the anesthesiologist know that at some time in the past I took this drug. We'll get into the side effects—immediate and long-term—to the "kill shit" treatment process later.

The regimen involves intravenous drips of the three drugs. The first week of a three-week cycle was every day for about four hours. The next two weeks were only an hour on Monday ("Bleo" day) with four three-week cycles initially planned. There were two additional chemo regimens as part of the protocol if this first one was unsuccessful, each one involving increasingly stronger drugs and ultimately requiring quality of life decisions by my family and me.

Having worked out the day I first met with Dr. Shu and run a 5K the day before (remember, I had no symptoms of the cancer), I had what nurses love: big, available veins. I was an "easy stick," as the nurses would say. It was easy to get a good IV going on me. By the end of chemo, I was somewhat of a "hard stick"; you are a pin-cushion for needles during this whole process. By the end of chemo, my veins had retreated (for fear, no doubt) and hid in an effort to avoid the needle. I was not able to do much of anything during this time: sit or nap on the couch, watch TV, and make a few phone calls—there was no way could I do anything more than that. I certainly could not work out or run. My body was wasting away under the onslaught.

I tolerated the first cycle of chemo fairly well. I was tired but able to work and function. My initial understanding was that if the chemo was successful, the testicle removal was considered "minor" surgery, and there was a possibility that the major tumor would shrink to nothing. Therefore, I kept working, hoping that I might be able to beat the cancer without the upheaval of disability and without stopping my practice.

What I found out soon after, however, was that even if the major tumor shrunk to nothing, Dr. Wang would remove the lymph nodes in the abdominal area as a precaution—a very major surgery. It would involve taking all my innards out, putting them on my chest or table, and retracting the tumor area. I would need to take time off work. As I explained to my partners and fellow therapists at the office, I had good disability insurance, or so I thought (more on that later). I also had a great life insurance policy; the building and practice would go on with or without me. To a person, my partners and colleagues were extremely supportive, an initial lesson in receiving and being loved that this whole experience gave me.

After a couple of weeks of chemo, John and Billy came down for fun, support, and to love on me. It was again a godly blessing. We laughed a lot and cried a little—just what I needed. We went to the beach, stayed in a hotel, and continued our mutual playful put-downs.

After a long day at the beach, I went back to the hotel and decided to take a shower. After I got out, I noticed the drain was backing up. I thought that strange for a nice hotel, but whatever. When I dried my hair, I realized it was coming out in bunches—I was the source of the drain backing up! I was surprised because for some reason the nurses told me from the beginning that they didn't think I would lose my hair with this type of chemo. Wrong! I suddenly entered the world of the great comb-over. It was becoming more urgent that I tell my clients before they could notice themselves. I also needed to face the music and pick a final date of work before going on disability. Stuff was happening pretty fast. Although appearance has always been important to me (partly why I run and work out), chemo soon gave me different priorities. It was paramount how I felt and no big deal how I looked. Other people had to deal with that. I could avoid the mirror if I wanted to.

In addition to the hair loss, my feet got numb, my legs itched, I had mouth sores, and I had sores on and great sensitivity in my hands and elbows, which was most painful. The toxic drugs were apparently settling in those areas.

After the first day or two of chemo, the skin around my shoulders and chest was very itchy, so naturally, I scratched—bad idea; I soon had bruised stripes all over my shoulders and chest. I looked like a tiger. They were still there two-plus years later.

Of course, the elbow and hand sores were unique to me, apparently. The doctor and nurses hadn't seen that reaction before. It got so painful that I dreaded turning a key in a lock or accidentally bumping my elbows on anything.

At the end of the second cycle, I decided to try and run to cleanse my system. Sweating has always been a powerful way for me to cleanse myself. Of course the "run" was more like a slow walk with a running motion because I had no energy and couldn't run or work out throughout the chemo process, but I was determined. To my pleasant surprise, the sweating helped release the toxins from my elbows. It came out in ugly-looking patches that, of course, the nurses had never seen before but was much relief for me from the pain.

My hands were less sensitive but still a problem. You could see the black marks of the chemo in my fingernails and toenails, and it would last for many months after chemo was complete. The foot numbness and itchy lower legs may be a permanent side effect as well. They represent some "minor" nerve damage.

One positive side effect was that several weeks after chemo ended, as my hair began to grow back (all over my body), my beard was almost a real beard. Before cancer, I had always had these little "Indian deserts," I called them. I have just enough Native American blood to mess up a decent beard and not enough for any school grants or casino money—typical me. But curiously, facial hair now grew in those deserts. Chris, my youngest son, was jealous because with the same genes, he had the same deserts. I suggested he could go through chemo to correct the problem. He declined the offer.

On three different occasions, my blood counts were so low that I couldn't even take the chemo. They just sent me home with the ominous warning that if I started bleeding or got a temperature to go straight to the hospital. Apparently, if these things occurred, my body had no capacity to resist them. During these times I was given the task of self-administering a drug called Neupogen. This stuff was geared to boost my blood and immune system so I could tolerate more poison. It involved five days of sticking a needle into my belly fat. The needles were very small—twenty-five gauge. This was relatively painless but clearly not fun. One time a nurse put an eighteen-gauge needle in my package of ten needles (five to draw the medicine out of the bottle containers and five to stick in my belly). They used two for each administration because the needle often got clogged with the rubber material used to seal the bottles. She did this with the best of intentions. She thought I would have an easier time getting the Neupogen out of the bottle with the bigger needle. The only problem was she didn't tell me and, of course, it was the very last needle in the bag. I had no choice but to use it on me. Now twenty-five and eighteen gauge may not seem like a big difference, but trust me; it looked like a harpoon! I jammed it into my belly. It only went in halfway and some blood squirted out. I wasn't happy as I jammed it the rest of the way in. I was fit to be tied. I later found out that because of the bigger needle, I probably stuck it past the intended fatty area and into my muscle. I guess I now have Neupogized stomach muscle.

Nonetheless, as it turned out, the "kill shit" philosophy was working. Halfway through the twelve-week regimen, I had another CT scan. The major tumor had shrunk to half its size, and the spots in the chest cavity were gone. It was the first good news we'd heard since the start of this whole nightmare. Six weeks of nightmare and now a ray of sunshine. We were encouraged.

The effects of chemo had an incredible impact. Although there is some knowledge by the professionals about expected side effects, everybody is unique, and they can't really predict how your body will respond or, in my case, what weird stuff my body would do with the poisons it took in. My hearing and eyesight got worse, which was aggravating to the kids sometimes because I really couldn't make out what they were saying with some cell phone calls. "What?" became one of my most frequently used words. I later was tested at Kaiser, after my recovery, and they recommended hearing aids in both ears! I chose to delay this inevitability, however.

More importantly, I had what is sometimes called "chemo brain." This involved sometimes subtle and sometimes clear indications that the poisons had run through my brain as well. It was like small, select areas of the computer motherboard of my brain had short-circuited. The best example I can give you is the phone conversation I had with a worker from the Social Security office. I was going to wait to apply because benefits were only payable after a year of disability, but I found out there was a death benefit if you died after six months—entirely possible in my case. Since the application process is arduous (it took me approximately ten hours online), I wanted to remove this headache from Denel and maximize her financial situation if I died. A couple of days after I completed the application, I received a call from the worker at the Social Security office. She told me that if I could answer a few simple questions, I wouldn't even need to go down to the office—a very desirable outcome. She asked me my father's first name. I quickly banged out, "Donald Francis Duprez." She asked me my mother's maiden name, "Bennett," and her first name, "Elizabeth." She asked me again, I said "Elizabeth." She stated, "That's not what we have down in our records." I was confused. I knew my mother-in-law's first name, Millie. I knew John and Billy's moms' first names, Dottie and Marvel, and I only saw them every couple of years. The worker said she would have to schedule an appointment in the office to reconcile the difference when I again said, "Elizabeth." At that point, Denel came into the study, not really knowing all that was going on but intuitively said, "Phyllis?" I was dumbfounded. Yes, my mom's name is *Phyllis* Elizabeth (Bennett) Duprez. I had a computer malfunction in my brain about my mom's first name! The chemo brain seems to be getting decidedly better as I get more and more distant, timewise, from the chemo. My wife and friends sometimes disagree, however. It is, at times, a ready-made excuse for any and all *faux pas*! Finally, a benefit from the nightmare!

Throughout the chemo, my spirits were greatly bolstered by family attendance at the actual chemo sessions. Denel, Nikki, Chris, and Gabe would visit, and we would watch movies, tell jokes, or they would keep me company while I slept. Kaiser provided either rooms or cubicles that afforded the participation of family.

The nurses were like angels. They were supportive, tender, responsive, and gentle, apologizing for IV sticks that were necessary and not their fault. Kaiser itself, as an organization, also did something that impressed us. With a dedicated nursing staff, chemo area, and pharmacist, there were no co-pays for all chemo treatments. This had to be expensive for them to provide, but it seemed compassionate of the organization to not require them. It was as if they were saying, "You are dealing with enough as it is," which was much appreciated.

There were tender and painful moments in this process as well. Chris, my then eighteen-year-old son, came down from Cal State Monterey Bay and sat through some chemo sessions with me. He turned away as he cried the first time he saw them start the IV. It was as if the reality hit him more so then, sweet but painful; he loves his Poppy. My daughter Nikki, so much like her dad with energy and drive, slowed down to be with me. I cherished that time, not knowing if those moments might be my last.

Chemo is horribly debilitating. Everything tastes odd, you are exhausted, you feel awful, your system is full of poison—there is no getting around it. Shit is being killed.

FIVE PUNCHES

The most painful thing, emotionally, through the entire diagnosis and treatment process was telling the people I loved the bad news. It literally tore my soul each time. I say "each time" because not only was I blessed to have twenty-plus family and friends near to my heart, but I also had about fifty clients I needed to tell.

Managing the feelings of others, as well as my own, was an emotional gauntlet. With family, I had to get ready each time. I needed some time to sit with Denel and let the news sink in before I could share it. I had to process, grieve, feel sorry for myself, and get angry. I needed time to get back up after being knocked down. With clients, I didn't have that option. One after another, I had to go through the process and stay balanced enough to remember that I was the therapist and their feelings had to take priority, ethically. I also needed to set up communication channels: Denel to tell her folks; Don to tell my other brothers, Mike and Tom; Billy to tell John; another friend Bill to tell other members of our church; but *I* had to tell my kids. I cry now as I write this; that pain is still fresh and deep.

What brought everything to the breaking point for me was the fact that the news kept getting worse. There were five separate times where we thought we knew what we were dealing with and we got worse news: from cancer to an inoperable tumor, from stage 2 to stage 3, from one type of cancer to two, from normal to abnormal tumor markers, and from progress in chemotherapy to stagnation and confusion. There was also a Tumor Board presentation by my doctors, which would determine the consensus course of treatment. You see, as always, I was unique, problematic, and complicated. They needed to put their heads together to determine how to proceed with me. Each time it was like getting punched, but I would recover in a couple of days and be ready to move on, to fight, to deal with it, but each time I had to tell my family, my kids. It was so painful to hear their pain and confusion. The first time I told Chris just how bad it was, he said, "But Dad, you are Superman. You can't be sick." We were both crying. Belinda had just lost her mom and Nikki was embarking upon her new life as an adult and college graduate—the timing seemed incredibly unfair. Would I be around for her wedding when she met the right guy? It was a flood of pain that happened five times over. Too, too much for me—too many tears. We only have one heart. How can it be broken five times?

With the fifth go around of this torture, I started crying in my oncologist, Dr. Shu's, office. He was, like many medical doctors, uncomfortable and quickly offered me Prozac. No problem; give me the pills, but where the hell is the bottom line? Give it all to me, and I can deal with it, but quit killing me a piece at a time! It was not within his power or mine. I had to take it as it came.

Throughout the process of the cancer, however, Denel and I never felt so loved. Family, friends, church members, and clients all came out of the woodwork to love on us. People were genuinely supportive. We had always been caregivers, and now the energy needed to be reversed, and it was. People offered many things and gave many things, but what I told everyone I wanted most were prayers and jokes. I got a whole basket full of funny cards. They were a joy to read and uplifting beyond comprehension. In the darkest moments, we could still find joy. My brother Mike was the most amazing in this area. He sent me literally dozens of cards. He loved me in the way I had asked. Thank you, Mikey. Our church brought us many meals, friends gave us many restaurant gift cards, and our pastors were supportive and available (thanks, Kevin and Jeff). The humor, food, and support were great, but the love was better. We truly felt loved. It made a huge difference.

Our church has a board, like most churches. When the board heard about my condition and how bad it was, thirty board members dropped to their knees and prayed for me. Although I was very touched that they did that, it also reminded me, oh yeah, I'm at Stage Toast. I hope they didn't hurt themselves dropping too quickly. I really was in dire need of help, and they knew it.

Sometimes in the course of a deep struggle, you meet additional problems and people who stand in the gap for you. I had a disability policy through the American Psychological Association for eleven years prior to my illness. From the first contact with the case manager of the company with which my policy was held, she was adversarial, ignorant, and malicious. She told me that if I used any other money to survive during my disability that they had the right to deduct that amount from my payments. That was horrifying since the amount I would be getting was about a third of my usual income and the only way we could survive financially was by using savings, retirement money, and Social Security. She told me three different times in a snotty tone, "Read your policy." I said I had read my policy and that clause about other income was not in there. Again, "Read your policy." After a couple weeks of sleepless nights and daily anguish (I'm a responsible guy, and my priority was that my family be okay, whether I was or not), I received a letter without any apology from the case manager stating that, indeed, I was correct. She had not apparently read *her* policy!

However, it wasn't over yet. She called me on the Wednesday before Thanksgiving to tell me that when my waiting period was up (mid-January) to receive benefits. They had determined, in their infinite wisdom and blatant self-interest, that I would *not* be disabled! I was flabbergasted. I asked her what she based that decision on, and she said since I had "finished" chemotherapy, and because she hadn't yet received the records from one of the doctors, they considered this grounds for dismissal of my case. Hmmm ... I was not done with chemo, and at that point in time, my tumor was still declared as inoperable, and I had two surgeries ahead of me, if not more chemo as well. I was outraged and determined to take it no more. I told her to never call me again and that I would only accept written communication from her. I spoke with her supervisor. He was appropriately attentive and agreed that if any urgent matter required verbal communication, he would be the contact person. I sent him copies of all correspondence just to make sure he fully understood what the case manager was doing. I also set about to find an attorney to protect my rights. The anguish this kind of behavior caused me is hard to describe. Injustice at any time is hard to tolerate, but in such a weakened and vulnerable state, it was unbelievable to me. It felt like violation upon violation. I was so vulnerable and felt so powerless. It felt truly cruel.

My buddy Billy has a great way of describing lawyers. With great disdain, he says, "They *produce* nothing." Well, I can't say I've had great experiences with attorneys myself, but I needed help, and I had to look somewhere. I contacted Mike Bidart, an attorney I had provided some expert testimony for years prior. He had already been very helpful with Denel's parents (for free!) regarding a tragedy they were involved with. He was again quite helpful with a referral to Jeff Rubin, an attorney out of Alaska who specialized in this kind of law. Jeff had very personal knowledge of cancer treatment. He was unbelievably helpful with both treatment resources and legal advice. Eventually, the insurance company saw the error of their ways, and legal action was averted. But these two attorneys helped restore, for me, a somewhat-tainted image for attorneys. Together they *produced* quite a bit of peace in me.

LEARNING TO RECEIVE

Denel and I are in the helping, healing profession. We have always been givers. For me, personally, I love to give. It feels especially meaningful when, whether it's children or clients, the gifts are valued and passed on. The gifts make a difference. I can even say I am most comfortable giving. Receiving has always been more difficult. Whether that's historical shame, unworthiness, or simply a control issue, receiving, celebrating, and winning have been lessons I've gradually learned through Denel's family. Denel will celebrate anything at the drop of a hat. She has taught me much that way. But cancer is the great equalizer, the great disabler, a great purity that puts you in need of others.

Having always been independent (I am American, after all) and hard working, I learned well how to work and struggle through life's challenges. I can even say I was quite good at it—probably too good. If I'm honest, life has been too much of a struggle for me. Acceptance, submission, and letting go (important aspects of a spiritual path) were never easy or fully engaged. If I just worked harder, did more of the same, I would persevere.

This paradigm simply does not fit the gift of cancer. It requires a whole new way of being—at least from how I had lived life. I now was the needy one, unequivocally, absolutely, without a doubt. Remember, this poor sucker was at Stage Toast. I had to learn how to let others do things for me, help me, love me. It was a total paradigm shift. I was facing death, not just struggling through life.

I was soon overwhelmed with immersion in the process. My family, my friends, my partners, my colleagues, and my clients genuinely cared, offered, and did things for me. The purity, the consistency, and the depth were truly touching. Now I don't necessarily advocate having others define for you what you need at this time. Those closest to me—Denel especially—could push through some residual resistance and see needs because they have a deep understanding of who I am. I had to begrudgingly listen at those times. Don also persistently asked, "Do you want me to come up there? I'll take off work and be up any time you need." I did need him to go with me to some appointments, the needle biopsy, etc., but I really needed him available for the surgeries and, if I didn't survive, to take on certain caretaking responsibilities with Denel, the kids, and the practice.

I also didn't want visitors during most of the three-and-one-half months of chemo. Prayers, jokes, and restaurant gift cards were wonderful. But I felt too miserable physically to want or be able to benefit much from visits. Even with people I really cared about, it was just more work than I could do. I had nothing to give. I was just trying to survive. I was very appreciative that there were those willing and, later when I felt better, able to visit me, but really I just wanted to sleep, rest, and have nothing more asked of me than to pass the time and get out of the chemo phase.

Denel is Italian in all the beauty and stereotype that implies. She is alive, full of zest for life, and joyful—unless she's agitated by a gnat or some challenge to her patience. A story I love to tell (she cringes when I tell it) is when we were first looking for a house in our city, Rancho Cucamonga. You may have heard of it if you are old enough to remember the Jack Benny skit about the train going to "Anaheim, Azusa, and Cucamonga!" Hey, I've lived in two of those cities. Anyway, we were driving around in this city (it was more of a rural town then—the "boonies," as my friend Ken would later say) when, after one hour—yes, *one* hour—she was discouraged because we hadn't found a house yet! I couldn't stop laughing. She laughs herself, but you get a picture of what a challenge patience can be for her at times. Throughout the treatment process, however, I would have to rely on her, depend on her, and at times give up control to her in ways that our relationship hadn't ever seen. Frankly, I was scared that I would be a burden to her so much so that it would overwhelm her. I guess I thought that there was a certain degree of Italianness—no matter how willing the human spirit—that even she couldn't overcome. I was quite wrong. She rose to the occasion. She was a patient, flexible, and great caretaker. The cancer forced her and helped her to find new ways to love me. She was a great blessing to me.

There were many people who were amazingly supportive as well. Gina, one of our partners, stepped up into the many roles I performed for our practice. She did this willingly and very skillfully. It was a true gift from her heart, and I appreciated her selflessness. Doug, our other partner, also filled in capably. Doug has a thought process unlike most—sometimes very insightful, sometimes just curious. He said, with the kindest intentions, I'm sure (and I took it that way), that I had the heart of a rhinoceros. Now I don't know much about the heart of a rhinoceros, and I've never heard it used as an analogy, but the kindness and respect were well received. When Doug later reviewed the book, he took it upon himself to explain his analogy in the form of a poem (see appendix B). A unique but much appreciated friend. Bill E., a church brother and friend, was also forever present, available, and willing to be in the communication conduit to others to relieve me in that area. His sense of humor was a great help. There are just too many others to mention, but they know they were there for me in a deeply uplifting way. I may have been dying at that point, but I was loved and blessed with many dear friends. As the psalmist said about God, "Even though I walk through the valley of the shadow of death, I will fear no evil, for you are with me," (Psalm 23:4, NIV). Well, I was plenty scared but also strangely peaceful with so many others walking with me. I was not alone in the valley.

Humor is a healing potion in this whole process. If we can't openly talk about cancer, especially with family, it's like the elephant in the room that everyone knows about and nobody acknowledges. Billy, with his unique sense of humor, came up with something that was very effective in dealing with this dynamic. He called it "playing the cancer card." If I wanted someone to do something for me or I wanted to avoid doing something or I just shamelessly wanted an oozing of pity/sympathy poured out, I would say things like, "Well, I'd do that, but I do have cancer, you know," or, "Maybe you didn't know, but I have cancer, and I just got out of surgery," or, "I would do that myself, but I'm pretty tired from the chemo, the cancer, and all the surgeries I've been through." Now these things were said with family and were so openly manipulative that they were ridiculous. What they did was allow everyone to laugh, acknowledge the elephant in the room, and *not* to pity me. It was open, funny, and is now a part of our conversations and play. It was, I think, a great relief for everyone involved. If you have an odd sense of humor like I do and your family knows that (my kids call me a "cornball" because of all my corny jokes), I would recommend playing the cancer card as a way to relieve the pressure and play with that elephant in the room.

Another lesson in receiving was brought about by the American Cancer Society (ACS). Denel and I have given to many charities consistently over the years. The need was now squarely with us. The ACS has a program that reimburses you for travel to doctor and chemo appointments. Since these were so many—often daily—and finances were tight, it was a welcomed relief. It was a unique and very pleasant surprise. It helped.

A word of caution about how you frame things is in order here as well. I had what the doctors called an "inoperable" tumor. This meant that, at present, it could not be taken out. There was, however, still hope that after chemo, it would shrink and then could be removed. I described this situation, I thought, completely to one adult client. His understanding, however, was not that I was at Stage Toast but that I was toast, period, and that I was definitely going to die. He told a friend and former pastor, Rob Acker, about this after church one day. Rob and his wife, Kathi, came to our house immediately and with, I'm sure, great apprehension about what they would find. I reassured them (somewhat) that, although true, there was still considerable hope. Their love and support were evident anyway and a great blessing to us.

Learning to receive is a lesson we are all learning in some capacity for the duration of our lives. It might mean learning how to accept help, how to believe and soak in affirmation, or letting people take care of us, but whatever the form, it is vital. We were not meant to live alone; we were meant for relationship, and whether we like it or not, relationships are built on the give *and* the take. It can't be all one or the other. We learn from each other how to do both, how to carry each other's burdens, how to work together. Even if this concept is a struggle at first, it ends up being one of life's greatest blessings when embraced. It was for me.

FAITH

As I had previously noted, the four years preceding the diagnosis of cancer were the worst of my life. Family tragedies, family struggles beyond our understanding, financial, and health and practice stressors had shaken our faith in a good God to the core. Spiritual truths we had lived by most of our lives seemed strangely out of sync with the realities we were experiencing. Frankly, we felt abandoned by God. There were times in the midst of these prolonged trials that I asked to be taken away, even demanded it. I was angry at God and not afraid to show it. Was the cancer God's answer?

The first couple of months after the diagnosis, especially with the worsening clinical picture and the residual wounds from the past four years, our faith was in a proverbial black hole. I had been taught by a former client, who was working his way through a twelve-step recovery program, what I thought was a beautiful prayer. He simply said "please" when he woke up in the morning and "thank you" at night before he went to bed. The simplicity and breadth of the process had always struck me as meaningful. I used that prayer during this time—not so much because I believed it was the best approach, but because it was all the spiritual energy I could muster. If you are still out there, Big Guy, I've got one fingernail left hanging on to the cliff. I have heard Luis Palau say that God has no grandchildren—that everyone, regardless of upbringing, will need to make choices about God as an adult. I feel this is true. We had raised Nicole with modeling of Christian love and basic training but knew that eventually she, Chris, Belinda, Gabe, and Angel, all our kids, would need to choose their own path, their own relationship with God.

Nicole, our Nikki, was twenty-two years old at the time I was diagnosed. She had just graduated from Azusa Pacific University (yeah, my alma mater) with a business marketing degree. She is exceptional at event planning and loves it. She has her dad's organizational and energy gifts and her mom's creativity and power gifts. She is a blessing to us. She is an amazing dynamo. Nikki had gotten involved with a large, apparently on-fire church in San Diego, where she moved (The Rock). She clearly was choosing her path and growing tremendously before our eyes. It was at this time that we got another lesson in receiving: Nikki carried us for several months spiritually when our faith was too encrusted with the current and recent pains we'd suffered to allow us to see the hand of God working. He was working through Nikki. She was so sure that I was going to be okay that she even had a hard time understanding our fears, anxiety, and faithlessness. She just couldn't relate. She felt the closeness of God, and all we felt was the chasm in the relationship.

After a few months of her carrying us spiritually, our faith slowly began to return. For me, with my prognosis down to about a 30 percent chance of survival, my faith was that God was good, that He was in charge, and that my family would be okay. This was a tremendous peace for me. I did not have faith in a particular outcome—that I would live. I didn't know what God's plan was; I just knew it would all be okay. If I died, I would have time for meaningful good-byes and closure with legacy issues resolved. My family and loved ones would be okay.

Eventually, my faith expanded to see the cancer as a gift. I have been working more than full time (plus school for many years) since I was eighteen years old. The cancer first forced and then, as I could appreciate it, allowed me to take six months off from my practice. During much of chemo, I was miserable, and recovering from two surgeries was no picnic. I had more joyful time with family, seen such growth in my children, and been loved on by so many people, all of which would not have happened without the cancer. It was a blessing. We were absolutely beaten by the prior four years, but God is never intimidated by the earthly score; two strikes, two outs, bottom of the ninth, He can still go yard (a baseball term for a home run). I guess that's the difference in Nikki's faith and mine. She was sure He would, and I was sure He could but didn't know if that was His plan, nor did I feel particularly worthy. Grace abounds, as we will see. I still don't know if Nikki's type of faith is better, deeper than mine. I just know that we both had the peace we so desperately needed, and we both felt God working.

I truly felt at peace. I didn't need God to make it turn out a certain way. I just desperately needed to know that He was in it. Was I already "in faith" at that point? I don't know. That's a question beyond my theological understanding. But once I knew God was in it, I could truly let go and trust Him. I guess that made my faith conditional, weaker, less pure. But so powerful is God's felt presence that it narrows the Kierkegaardian leap of faith necessary to bridge the gap between what we can prove and what we choose to believe. The gap was now short enough that even a spiritual weakling like me could bridge it. We can't prove God exists in any complete, external way, but we can know He is there in us, with us, for us, and in control. That which He wants the most—our will, our soul, our person—has to be given up as a choice. I had to truly let go. It wasn't my life anymore. It was a beautiful peace at the end of a long, drawn-out boxing match that I had lost horribly, and I gained a peace that made no worldly sense—a peace that transcends all understanding (Philippians 4:7).

Unfortunately for me, and maybe most of us, it was necessary that my life be broken into so many pieces before I could truly give it up. Maybe true saints are those who can let go *before* there is nothing left to hold on to. Those, unlike the Apostle Thomas, can believe and live accordingly without seeing the nail holes in Jesus's hands, and, unlike Saul (Paul), let go/make major changes in their life course without a dramatic and direct intervention from above. In this regard, who are you? Hebrews 11:1 (NIV) states, "Faith is being sure of what we hope for and certain of what we do not see."

Nikki and I were both now sure of what we hoped for and certain of what we couldn't see, even if those hoped for things were very different. We both had faith. The current crisis now had purposeful, meaningful mystery for me. But I still could not make sense of the prior four years of torment. Remember, for Denel and me, the four years *before* the cancer were hell on earth. They made no sense. But the following two verses, when put together, plus the peace of God's presence in the cancer struggle, gave me a sense that I didn't have to understand it all *now*. It just didn't hold the value or importance to me anymore—just a valley before a mountain. James 1:2 (NIV) says, "Consider it pure joy, my brothers, whenever you face trials of many kinds because you know that the testing of your faith develops perseverance," and Romans 5:3–5 (NIV) says, "And perseverance character, and character hope and hope does not disappoint us."

Hope is a beautiful chalice we fill with our deepest dreams, and God is the best completer of those dreams, not us. He is the best "closer" there is. Hope is thus always looking upward. It is a reconnection to God.

SEX

As I've said, chemotherapy is devastating to the body. You are hurt, exhausted, and bruised from the inside out. Sex is not a top priority. Given the rather personal nature of testicular cancer, it was even more of an issue for me. What I looked like, how I felt, could I transfer any cancer to Denel by having sex, etc.—these were all concerns I was having. I wasn't sure, and I wasn't going to take a chance. But I also had some fairly deep questions about my "manhood." Would I ever be normal again? Given the natural progression of sex in most marriages, early on I earned some hero-type partnering points for my sexual prowess (rare, I admit, but it did happen on occasion. Denel can't remember, but I can!). With small children, hero-type partnering points shifted from sexual activity to my willingness to help with the laundry and diapers on the weekends. At this point in our relationship, although we are still sexually active (when she's awake and I'm not exhausted), I earn hero-type partnering points by spotting a Starbucks before she does in our travels. This natural progression, the results of surgery, and chemo fit quite nicely into Denel's needs but not necessarily mine.

Dr. Wang was very open about surgeries and letting us ask questions. We were generally well prepared. However, for the first surgery, which involved the removal of my right testicle, the fact that my scrotum would be shaved of all hair never came up. So coming out of the shower after this surgery was somewhat embarrassing. Bald heads have become fashionable, and I could fit right in there, but a hairless scrotum was not a pretty sight, at least in my eyes. Now Denel is gentle and kind generally but quite willing to be honest. I know when she's blowing smoke in my direction, it doesn't last long. What she said surprised me, but I can see where it might be true. She said most women don't like male pubic hair; it's kind of gross and gets in the way! I chose to believe her. Check with your wife; we might start a new fad here.

So now I had two of the three things that made our sex life better for Denel: I was hairless, and my libido was reduced. It matched hers. Now for the *coup de gras*—the major surgery. The second one of the two involved an incision from my xiphoid process (the little bone at the base of the ribs that is used to mark off CPR compressions) to about three or four inches below my belly button, about twelve to fifteen inches total. Dr. Wang even showed us exactly where the incision would be. It was at this time that he also informed me that he would have to cut a nerve that would prevent me from ejaculating in sex! Wait a minute; isn't death better? He went on to somewhat relieve my anxiety by saying that since I could still experience sex as I normally had, I would not develop the proverbial "blue balls" guys dread with the build up associated with an absence of sex and I would essentially ejaculate air! Okay, this is too much to comprehend and quite alarming when I noticed a slight grin on Denel's face. She now had me exactly where she wanted me: hairless, decreased libido, and ejaculating air! No more messy fluids to deal with for her. Our sex life would change drastically for me, possibly be okay, but she was elated! I may have stumbled upon the solution to the age-old conflict between the sexes—if guys would just shave their pubic hair, decrease their libido, and ejaculate air, the divorce rate would plummet! I suspect I'll get few followers to this plan, however.

Mr. Babcock, Dr. Wang's physician's assistant, was more realistic about sex after surgery. He said, "No, it won't be the same." He was closer to the truth. Although sex was changed for me, it was still possible and a part of our lives together. It was not ideal but still good, especially thanks to that little blue pill! After the removal of the testicle, I would be somewhere between a man and a woman, I guess. I would not be a eunuch because I would still have one testicle, but I would be as it says about eunuchs in Isaiah 56:3 (NIV), "I am only a dry tree." I guess a living dry tree is better than a dead tree, after all. Whatever illusions and fantasies (delusions?) I had tried to hold on to (imagine?) about my sexual prowess, I would be, at best, Puff the Magic Dragon. I could only hope that, if I survived, "little Denel Duprez would love that rascal, Puff."

"MINOR" SURGERY

The original site of the cancer was my right testicle. It had to be removed. The normal protocol for my type and stage of cancer would have been to remove the testicle first, chemotherapy next, and then the major surgery later to remove any remaining tumor(s). With my case, however, since the cancer was so advanced and the largest tumor was inoperable, it was critical to start the chemo first and deal with the surgeries later.

Having completed one round (four cycles—three and a half months in total) of chemo, it was time to remove the testicle. Now any guy approaching this type of surgery has got to be apprehensive, if not scared out of his mind. But to make matters even worse, Dr. Wang described this as "minor" surgery. "Minor" wasn't a description unique to me, although some friends might disagree. It was what Dr. Wang called the surgery. Please, no guy in the world would call the surgical removal of one of his testicles a minor matter. It just isn't so. But I'm stuck with medical definitions.

Denel had a sense that it wasn't minor. In a sweet gesture at home prior to the surgery, she kissed the testicle good-bye. It was funny and sweet—her own idea. There is a famous announcer's phrase in baseball related to a homerun: "It's a deep fly ball ... going, going, gone! You can kiss that ball good-bye. Home run!" Well, it was very much a sweet gesture—certainly a home run in my book. Denel kissed that ball good-bye!

The surgery itself was meant to be one and a half hours with a return home the same day. I guess in those terms it's minor, but I still can't buy that descriptor. Sorry, it wasn't minor to me. Well, at least the procedure didn't involve cutting the scrotum. They actually make about a four-inch incision in the groin just below the waistline and pull the testicle out. I was actually pleased with that procedure with the hopes my scrotum would be relatively untouched and at least not cut. That promised an easier healing process in my mind.

As I said previously, however, there was no mention of a shaved scrotum area. I had assumed, reasonably from my perspective, that no cutting meant no shaving. Whether this was just a vengeful nurse or really necessary, I don't know, but I was stuck with the consequences. Chris was empathic and seemed to identify with me as he said as I was rolled down for surgery, "Stay strong, Dad." I soon discovered that there is a reason for pubic hair: everything sticks together if there isn't any. People thought I walked like a cowboy after the surgery because of tenderness or pain—no, it was for want of baby powder! Again, the series of indignities seemed endless. Denel uses baby powder. I felt like I was somewhere in the twilight zone between losing my manhood and becoming a woman.

Further proof of my confusion was the fact that I felt right at home within a very female conversation a few weeks later. Denel, her best friend Denise, and Denise's mom, Sheila, and I were all in a car together. I guess the mere fact that I was in a car with three women and this didn't seem odd to me was some verification of the changes I was enduring. For some reason they started having one of those female conversations that never occur in mixed company. Honest, raw girl talk ("angry vaginas") and other funny, weird, and pretty personal stuff. The kind of talks guys never hear and have themselves (guy talks) only over a couple of beers. You know what I'm talking about here. Well, what was surreal is that they didn't seem to pull any punches with me there and I felt right at home. After we left the car, I said, even to my surprise, "You know I wouldn't have been comfortable with that conversation if I still had two testicles"; they fell down laughing. It was like I was the first *unwilling* recipient of a sex-change operation! What with the lotion now necessary for my dry skin because of the chemo, the necessity of baby powder after the first operation, almost having to use Denel's blood (she gave blood before one of the surgeries, same blood type, in case it was needed), and my bizarre comfortableness with raunchy female conversations, it was all a challenge to my sense of my manhood.

The indignities didn't stop, even after the whole experience. Nikki chose to study church discipleship and music for a year in Australia at Hillsong International Leadership College. Part of our support for her was my driving and making the payments on her car. The fact the car had a personalized license plate that read "GRL4JC" and had a dancing girl sticker on the side window was further grist for the humiliation mill from friends and family. Even worse, I got a lot of young guys pulling up alongside me in a flirtatious manner with full expectation of a seeing a young girl driving. Wouldn't you? Seeing this old guy instead was really a shock, I'm sure! Chris was able to frame the experience in positive terms for me. He took an optimistic perspective and said, "Dad, your sack isn't half empty. It's half full." Hey, thanks, son; that helps … a little, I guess, maybe … not so much.

Being a therapist, there are also advantages to my new status. There is an inherent problem of triangulation when working with couples that can be difficult to overcome in some client's minds. This refers to the reality that there will always be two male or two female points of view compared to one of the other depending on the gender of the therapist. Well (trust me, I wouldn't actually share this with a client), I now have a unique perspective, "gonadically speaking" halfway between the two gender points of view. Again, I may have solved a therapeutic problem for therapists working with couples, but I expect few would be willing to pay the price for this neutrality. Wimps!

My buddy Billy is a creative guy with a vivid imagination. He has helped me greatly with names for my new status: "one ball man"; "have some ball"; "cajon"; "family jewel"; the baseball phrase umpires shout to start a game, "play ball"; other guys get their balls busted; just one for me, etc. Of course, all these terms are a lot funnier to him than they are to me, but I can admit they have a humorous side. I did start feeling that I was leaning to the left after the surgery. And some phrases that guys regularly use no longer applied to me—i.e., "Why, I'd give my right nut for_____." I'd already given my right nut and for nothing!

Billy and I also had some fun describing Dr. Wang's hypothetical experience during the surgery. I told him that Dr. Wang injured himself performing the surgery. Of course, Billy quickly chimed in, "What, did he hurt his eyes trying to see that little thing?" "No," I said, "he injured his back pulling that huge thing out of there. I told him beforehand to lift with his legs, but he didn't listen to me." Billy's version was probably closer to the truth, but it doesn't really matter at this point, now does it?

I did have plans to keep the testicle in a jar or something, but the pathologist needed it. I even had the fantasy after seeing some jellyfish on the beach at Pismo that I would take a big chunk out of one of them and send it to Billy and John. They usually don't appreciate that kind of humor much. At least they didn't when I sent them a full-sized color photo of my colonoscopy. But I enjoy it enough for all of us.

Oh yes, I almost forgot one more indignity. The preparation for the surgery involved marking the testicle with a magic marker—twice, honestly. The nurse informed me of her need to do this and thankfully offered the honor to Denel. She asked if she could make a happy face on the testicle and was told quite emphatically, "No."

Apparently this had actually occurred in the past, and when the surgical staff performed the surgery, they thought that the happy face was for the good testicle and took the wrong one out! Oops! So Denel could only mark or initial it. She chose to use my initials. Unfortunately, this was not the end. Dr. Wang still had to initial the testicle, that poor thing, resulting in me being exposed twice in the waiting room. Whatever sense of pride I might have had up to that point was quickly dissipating, I assure you.

The surgery went smoothly. I went home with a four-inch scar and healed up pretty quickly. I was feeling better and better every day away from chemo. Surgeries are a piece of cake compared to chemo.

SAYING GOOD-BYE

There is a beauty in sadness purely felt. There is a beauty in death if directly faced. Death is the great prioritizer. What is and is not most important becomes pretty clear when your chances of living are down to 30 percent. We are all going to die. The only question is when. This reality can help us to truly live, and it is part of God's plan. He set it up where this existence on earth is temporary—a working out of our relationship to Him, others, and ourselves. Now it may or may not be part of His plan for you or me at this time in our lives to die, but only He knows that.

My faith had grown sufficiently, as I approached the major surgery, that I had a blessed peace. Not only was I at peace with whatever happened, live or die, I can truly say at that point the cancer was a gift. I had seen so much growth in my kids, had more quality and quantity time with my family and friends, had been loved on by so many people, and had set up things for the well-being of my family if I wasn't around that I could fully see all the blessings the cancer had brought. During the times after chemo and between surgeries, I had even felt good, could work out, and could run again. I felt good enough to be obnoxious. I am unique, I guess, that way. When I feel really good, I'm the Pun Man. I have tons of playful energy to harass those I love. I punch my brother Don unceasingly but lovingly (he tolerates this well, but he could crush me if he wanted to).

In short, I am obnoxious. I enjoy it to no end. Those who are my targets often wished I were more tired and it would end. John came down, and we went to Pismo Beach (Kon Tiki Inn, my favorite) during one of these times. He was loving and supportive, and I was joyfully ripping on him relentlessly. What a blast for me. He said it well when he said to Denel, "I'm sending out all this love and I'm not feeling it coming back." It was, just in my weird way. It felt so good to feel good again—even if briefly in preparation for the major surgery.

Being somewhat obsessive-compulsive (my colleagues would enhance the "somewhat"), I needed closure. I had to know that I tied up as many loose ends for Denel and the kids as I possibly could. She had already buried one husband suddenly, tragically, and at way too young an age. If this was necessary again, I was determined that there would be nothing unclear for her to deal with. With as much support as I could muster, I planned everything foreseen in a structured way beforehand. I even went so far as to set up the cremation service to be used and designated where I wanted my ashes spread. Having a business, a practice, and multiple mortgages, our finances were a complicated behemoth. I manage the finances for Denel and I, and it is a large job that she would not want or enjoy. Her quality of life is very important to me. I needed to set things up so she could manage them with as little grief as possible. I felt I owed that to her. To accomplish this goal, I detailed all the information in writing and gave it to Don. He was also willing to be put on our business checking account. I wrote a good-bye letter to my family and friends and taped it (see "Celebration" chapter), complete with music dedicated to each person. I wanted a joyful celebration type of service if I didn't make it. I wanted Nikki to make some kind of display board for the funny cards I'd gotten and another for some very meaningful things that had been written to and by me over my life. I gave all this information to Don and Billy. When I called Billy into my study to walk him through all this stuff, he said, "Is this going to make me cry?" No, it was sad stuff but good stuff. I wanted to finish the race the way I'd always run it: with as much integrity and responsibility for all those I loved as I could muster. I wanted to finish strong.

The things I wrote came from deep within my soul. It took a while to formulate what I wanted to say. It involved a lot of tears and a lot of sleepless nights. Because it meant so much peace for me, I probably shared too much of this process with Denel. She needed me to survive. I needed closure. She didn't have the same peace about either way it turned out that I did. That was a mistake. However, after it was clear that I was going to make it, she said she couldn't help herself—she knew it would hurt, but she read the good-bye letter anyway. It did hurt, but she also knows that is me, and she got another picture of just how much I love her. She is my soul mate. In Pismo Beach early after the diagnosis, I told her that no matter what happened I would take care of her. She said she knew that after dating me a couple of months. Wow, she sure kept those cards close to the vest. I didn't think she fully trusted me until about seven years into our marriage! She worked that angle awfully well!

Having the peace I had about the outcome, many people asked if I wanted them to pray over me. This is a Christian tradition involving the laying on of hands in an effort to harness the power of the Holy Spirit for healing purposes. I welcomed all prayers but didn't feel a great need for this since I felt that God was already on board and at the helm. However, Denel wanted, maybe needed, me to go through this process. We set up a session with three pastors of a local church (Water of Life) where a friend, Linda Jones, was a minister. They were gracious, clearly godly, and quite supportive. In addition to the prayers and laying on of hands, they asked me to recall and let go of resentments I had toward people. I was surprised how many people came up. I can hold resentments pretty well and justify the reasons self-righteously quite well—another gift of mine, not such a good one. They asked if I felt any physical changes—I had some warmth in my abdomen, but otherwise unremarkable.

When we subsequently got the last CT scan before the major surgery, Denel was disappointed—me too, but less so—that the tumor had not shrunk any further from the chemo or the prayers. It was still half the original size but no smaller from the decrease measured at the halfway point through the chemo. I had a notion that the tumor might still have been impacted by the chemo and the prayers, even if it hadn't shrunk. As it later turned out, it was dead. Whatever killed it— prayers and/or chemo—had done the job well. But we wouldn't know the status of the tumor until after the major surgery.

It was likely that as many as two more rounds of chemo might also be necessary. These additional rounds of chemo would be with yet stronger drugs, the third round even what they termed "massive doses of drugs that would literally take me to the brink of death, if not over it." This last round of chemo was called "salvage chemo." As you can guess from the name, it's a last ditch medical effort to salvage a life at great risk to killing the person receiving it. This, for me, would involve quality of life decisions. I was determined to do everything correctly to maximize my chances of living, but I had a peace about dying, if that was the plan, and I had limits about what kind of torture I would put myself and my family through to hold on to this life.

I had decided, with Denel's knowledge and understanding, that I had limits to how far I would go into the "kill shit" model of care. If necessary, I would start the second round of chemo. This round would involve a very powerful drug called Ifosfamide (pronounced "ifosfa-oh, hide from this shit" in Jerry Latin). I was willing to commit to two cycles of this regimen (six weeks). If I could tolerate it, I would complete the regimen. If I could not, I would stop, do every homeopathic approach we could find, but otherwise enjoy what time I had left on this earth. I was categorically unwilling to even attempt the third regimen of massive doses. I've known too many people who have spent their last weeks and months of life on this earth semiconscious in an oncology unit instead of in God's country somewhere with loved ones. Not me. Denel respected my decision. I told Don, Billy, John, and Lee, my son-in-law. It was not a topic much discussed with the kids. Peace and selfishness is a gray area where quality of life and these kinds of choices are involved.

MAJOR SURGERY

Chemo done, "minor" surgery done and recovered from, it was now time to prepare for the major surgery that would go after the once-inoperable, still-remaining tumor in the lymph nodes behind my stomach. The tumor was now half its original size—seventeen centimeters—but still large. Worse, the cancer had spread to very sensitive areas involving veins and arteries to major organs: vena cava, aorta, etc. Dr. Wang (and Dr. Jerry) did not want to have to take the significant risks involved in trying to remove tumor material in this area. It was just too dangerous—loss of vital organs, loss of life, etc.

In Job 26:6 (NIV), it states that, "Death is naked before God." Well, I wasn't totally there yet, but literally and figuratively, I was down to my boxer shorts. Dr. Wang, as he had on several prior occasions, called me several days before the scheduled appointment with him to discuss options. Knowing my abhorrence of chemo and willingness to take my chances with surgery, he had already picked out a possible date. This was one of my other concerns. The surgery was expected to take eight hours. I was afraid that, as busy as he was, I might have to wait weeks or months before he would have an entire day available for the surgery. He had a day clear (or cleared it) in less than two weeks—another blessing. His willingness to call ahead and having a date already in mind were very helpful in allowing us to set up family support for the surgery date. We can't thank him enough.

The morning of the surgery, I was feeling genuinely at peace. I had peace with whatever the outcome was. Granted, I was more than ready to get it over with, but I was at peace. Denel drove me to the hospital at the crack of dawn, and it was just about time. Our friend Maggie had shared a comforting vision she had within a week or so prior to the surgery with Denel. She saw an angel holding both me and Denel, and she felt peace. Denel shared this with me, and it was somewhere in the back of our minds that morning.

Now if you don't have a sense of how weird I am by now, let me give you another dose. I knew that eight-plus hours of waiting in a room at the hospital would be a grueling experience for my family and friends. I had the idea, which tickled me pink, that the guys (and any of the gals who wanted to) should play poker during the surgery. I got fifty dollars in quarters and asked each guy to bring a five-dollar bill as a buy in. My plan was to have the deal rotated and for the dealer to play my hand. I hoped to wake up to some sympathy winnings of some sort, or at least everyone would have some fun passing the time. Either way it was good stuff.

In addition, Maggie brought a relative plethora of games and food for everyone; she earned her sainthood that day—well, at least from that latte-sipping group. Together with the poker, her gifts apparently helped considerably. At least so I was told later, as I was otherwise occupied at the time. Maggie also contributed greatly by being my so-called good-luck charm: every time she stood in as "me" during the poker game, she managed to win! Whether it was beginner's luck or some other divine connection, we'll never know. But what counts is, thanks to her, I constantly won throughout the day. Somehow I think I was smiling on that operating table simultaneously with each victorious play in my honor.

What's more, in honor of me, and without my prior knowledge, the poker players all decided to cheat as a testimony to me. Now let me explain. I am not a cheat, but I used to play this game within a game with my daughter Belinda and my mom. We would play cards together, I would try to cheat, and they would try to catch me. I didn't care whether I won; that wasn't the point. It was just the fun of the process and part of that weird, obnoxious nature of mine. One time Belinda and Grandma actually got a little perturbed and asked me to stop. I did. Within ten minutes, they realized in comparison the game was boring, and they asked me to cheat again so they could try to catch me! Like I said, I know I'm a pretty weird duck.

One of the things Dr. Wang wanted me to do was to give my own blood prior to the surgery. Since he was expecting an eight-hour surgery, he was predicting the need for blood—made sense but a little scary. We were going to try to get family to donate (he wanted two units, and there was only time enough for me to give one safely), but there just wasn't time to get blood types and donate with all the kids living in other cities. Fortunately, Denel had the same blood type, and she was able to give a unit as well. I guess I was now literally draining her of her lifeblood, not just by being needy and obnoxious. Since her Italianness permeates her being, I was concerned and joked about talking with my hands when I got out of surgery. (Through the years we've joked that we really only have one brain between us and, with chemo, maybe more like three-fourths of a brain.) Having her blood in me literally seemed like more of my progression away from manhood and into womanhood but still all good.

In an effort to hopefully avoid the surgical knife in the sensitive area around the veins and arteries, Dr. Wang planned to do several pathology samples during surgery. His thinking was that if the cancer material was essentially dead, he could leave this area alone—an outcome we both were hoping for. Well, the eight-hour surgery took ten and a half hours. The supporters waiting in the lobby apparently did pretty well for eight-plus hours, but then Denel started to melt down. Nikki felt prompted to pray, and another dear friend, Kathi Acker, whose husband, Rob, had been our pastor and still was our friend, asked the kids to physically support Denel. They went outside and prayed. Don—the Rock, the Duke of Big, the guy the VA should study for hardiness after a very active tour in Vietnam with the Americal Division—was his usual self through about hour nine. At that point, from what I'm told, he had a death stare on the door waiting for the doctor to come in. It was all getting a little too real for everybody. Of course, Billy, the eternal optimist, saw the length of time as a good sign—they were being thorough.

Who knows the truth, but it was scary, emotionally, for everyone and probably even more grueling for my body. But it was the next step toward really knowing where I stood. I could only hope it was the final step. In all likelihood, I at least was looking at more chemo. The thinking goes that even if the cancer is dead and removed, if they find even one live cancer cell, then further chemo is necessary and warranted. That looked like the best possible outcome I could hope for. If I even made it out of the ten-and-a-half-hour surgery alive, that is.

RECOVERY MIRACLE

"Hi, honey. You did really good. We have really good news. It was all scar tissue." After the ten-and-a-half-hour surgery and more time in post-op, Denel greeted my foggy brain with the great news. My first words were "Thank God." My next words almost immediately following were a plaintive about the next step: "Chemo?" No more chemo, no more surgeries. All our prayers were answered in the affirmative. Thanks, Big Guy!

All the pathology reports during the surgery had come back negative for any live cancer cells. The tumor was what they called "fibrous." It had, essentially, already been killed by the prayers and/or the chemo. It just didn't shrink any more after the initial decrease in size. What's more, I didn't (or couldn't) move my hands as I spoke because neither my or Denel's blood was necessary despite the length of the surgery—miracle upon miracle. I was in pain, but with a morphine drip, it was tolerable.

The hardest part of the recovery in the hospital was getting in and out of bed to walk—that hurt. I also had these weird (what would you expect of me?), uncontrollable spasms in my stomach area every time Dr. Wang, Mr. Babcock, or the nurses touched the area, which was often. But it too passed after a few days. I was determined to do as many laps as possible around the ward so I could go home. I was blessed with some good nurses, but Denel is the best nurse.

What was still critical was the final, full official pathology report. If all was not clean, I might have still needed more chemo. True to form, Dr. Wang brought a copy of the report in to me earlier than expected. The report showed that everything was clear; no cancer detected. Time to get my lazy butt (learned behavior) into the swing of things! Dr. Wang really seemed happy for us. He celebrated the victory with us. I had asked him some hard, direct questions over the course of the treatment process. If I was terminal, I wanted to know it. It would help my planning, and I wasn't afraid— "Don't hold back with me please." He was always straight and professional, but he seemed to genuinely care also. We have been blessed in so many ways.

Kaiser is an HMO. I work with managed care insurance companies and full well know the games that are often played to deny care. We received excellent overall care from the Kaiser system and very personally appreciated acknowledgements of our unique needs by many different doctors and nurses. One of the items on my things-to-do list as I was recovering was to give back, to acknowledge the excellent care and those special people who were so instrumental in my recovery. It isn't much, but I wrote a letter to Kaiser toward the end (see Appendix A). I have joked throughout this book a lot about names and less-than-optimum events, but the reality is, especially through Dr. Wang and the oncology nurses, we were blessed. We received exceptional care, and it saved my life.

The next phase had to do with walking a lot—boring but necessary. Lee, my son-in-law, noticed the track I was burning into the backyard grass as I walked to the back wall for up to twenty laps at a time, several times a day. I have had so little control over anything in this whole process that I wanted this: to walk as much as I could, to recover as fast as I could, to have choices again. I was exhausted and uncomfortable, but the pain quickly subsided. I was soon walking the 5K I used to run before the diagnosis and planning to work out as well (Dr. Wang said I had to wait six weeks before I could run or lift).

Of course, I was also looking forward to going back to work. With strong support from Belinda, Nikki, and Chris, Denel set herself up as the schedule police. This meant that once we agreed on a reasonable schedule, she would enforce it. This was intended to bring her peace and me healing by making sure that I didn't work too much, too long, or too hard. We had spent all of our savings and a big chunk of our retirement to survive during the six months I was off work (I had worked the first six weeks of chemo). I felt a need to get back to work at prior work levels to get us back above water financially, not the priority for the aforementioned people, however. Denel, I think, sort of relished this role and approached it with significant vigor. She likes to be directive, and she had me in a weakened state.

Besides, she had endured the most and worst with me, and I owed her some concessions anyway. We agreed to a slightly reduced schedule that involved more sleep, more rest, and fewer financial responsibilities. I was also committed to eating healthier since I had discovered a liking for salads and had gotten some education on acid/pH levels in my system (I was all acid and didn't even register on the paper used to measure pH levels!).

Oddly enough, for the first time in my life, I was actually able to gain weight, to get fat. I have never been able to get over 173 pounds my whole life. Although many envy this condition/metabolism, it was a real hindrance to trying to play linebacker at APC. I was a true lightweight—a boy among men—in that setting. Well, Nikki joyfully noticed one day my widening rear end. I had ballooned up to 185 pounds, as my metabolism hadn't apparently kicked in during the post-major surgery recovery. With great glee, she called me "Big Booty" (and still does in memory at times). Later, nearly two years after surgery, she noticed these two little pouches of fat on either side of my belly button, one being bigger than the other. Despite stomach workouts, I couldn't get rid of those. The bigger one was where I'd stuck the "harpoon" needle of Neupogen. I don't know, but between the surgery and the Neupogen, I now had what Nikki said looked like a small rear end in the front. She dubbed it "Little Booty" and enjoys her names for my physical anomalies often. I guess for both Nikki and Denel, seeing me with some unsightly fat was cause for celebration! They have always envied my metabolism, I guess.

I also was searching for the deeper meaning to the whole experience. What did God want me to learn from all this, and was I supposed to live differently? Certainly trusting Him more and worrying less, but was there more? There is a peace that comes with having faced death. It is a grounding experience that brings a unique clarity, something maybe Don has had after Vietnam. A lot of the white noise of life fades away. I know more deeply and more clearly what is important and what is not. I doubt this feeling will be richly with me from here on out. I'm sure I will get lost many times with life's trivial stressors, but, as I've said to many clients about different insights they've achieved, it is always easier to get back to something you've known than to find it the first time. I have found something, hard-earned, and I will cherish it. Thank you, Lord.

RECOVERY PROCESS: LIVING WITH THE BLESSINGS OF LIMITS

We, mostly me, now entered a different phase. We were all tremendously relieved at the miraculous outcome. But Denel and I have to continue to live with limitations and uncertainty. Given the course we'd already been on and the alternatives, these issues were joyfully approached. However, the limitations (sexual, energy, future work schedules, ongoing side effects of the chemo, etc.) were significant. The overall uncertainty of the cancer returning was also present, but, in truth, this is a reality that we all have to live with, not just cancer survivors. To heighten the uncertainty for us was the fact that part of the cancer was left untouched. This was due to the sensitivity of certain areas where cancer was, including those of vital veins and arteries. It is still in my body. We were banking on the pathology reports that it was all dead and not wanting the risk of death or vital organ loss with the scalpel.

The uncertainty of life itself, no matter what our circumstances, is true for us all. If you focus too much here, it will immobilize you. If you deny it, you can spend your life in empty pursuits that result in remorse and regret as you exit this life. If you hold this reality *and* have the courage to live fully anyway, it can help you prioritize and live more passionately and meaningfully. It is all a gift, even "bad" days. It can give you a sweet focus on the now with a predictable emphasis on relationships and people versus things and accomplishments—a deeper, better orientation to a life well-lived.

Cancer recovery has its own vocabulary. "Remission" is a term meaning there's no cancer present or growing *that they know about.* Hence, it's really good news but reflects the reality that medical knowledge of *your* body is always limited. "Cure" is only used after a number of years (often five plus) where no signs or symptoms of the cancer have been detected. Again, the limitations of medical science are felt firsthand. This forces you to live with the uncertainty of it all. However, uncertainty, as I've said, is true for us all in this life. What cancer survivors have is a crucible experience for appreciating this reality and all the blessings of life. For a time, they appeared to be ending for us.

Some cancer researchers speak of "rite of passage" phases to cancer. The first phase, separation, involves diagnosis and the initial designation of having cancer. You are, in some ways, uniquely separate from others and even your old cancer-free self. You are forever changed. The next phase, which includes treatment, is called liminality. It involves a threshold of change, the betwixt and between limbo state of treating an illness. You are ill, not well, but hopefully moving toward recovery and remission, but nobody really knows for sure. You are neither this (well) nor that (ill) but somewhere in between with a layer of hope. The final phase in a recovery process (as opposed to death) is reincorporation. Here is where you resume your life, reconnecting with functional and meaningful roles and activities, but you are in a forever altered state. You will, thankfully, never be the same again. In a practical way, we came upon this phase with my planned return to work. As I've said, having spent all of our savings and a big chunk of our retirement to survive during the six months off work to receive the most intense elements of the cancer treatment, I was anxious to begin a financial/security recovery process for my family.

Being a responsible guy, I tend to carry the financial well-being of my family in a 24/7, ever-aware vigilant state. Denel, bolstered by many family and friends, set herself up as the watchdog for my compulsive work tendencies. We began to negotiate about my return to work date and my work schedule after my return. I wanted more; she wanted less—you get the picture. She grounded me.

Dr. Wang said I might be able to return to work in as little as six weeks after the major surgery. Denel wanted nine; we settled on seven. We agreed I would have no more 7:00 a.m. appointments for clients, would take two hours off during my long work days, and would reduce my total hours by five. A therapist who needs such external structure to take care of himself may not be a pretty picture, but hey, I was a fifty-seven-year-old who was still growing up! A life of more trust and balance was necessary, appropriate, and still somewhat resisted but good for me. Sometimes blessings have to be forced down my throat. This was one such occasion, and Denel seemed to joyfully engage the process. Have you ever felt your spouse *enjoyed* rubbing your nose in something? Well, in this case, Denel was correct, and she'd earned the right for a measure of control. We'd been through hell together.

In addition to walking with me throughout all the painful setbacks, Denel shared with me after the recovery an especially poignant struggle she'd had. Being exhausted and bald from chemo, I would generally go to bed before her. She said afterward that it was very hard emotionally to get into bed with me. I was bald and decimated. It was like getting into bed with a dying man. I understand. She's been through an ordeal herself.

REVISITING THE VALLEY OF THE SHADOW OF DEATH

After all the treatment and recovery miracles, coupled with the ongoing physical limitations/damages/residue left over, comes the critical step of your first CT scan. Mine was scheduled for three months after recovery from surgery. The CT scan is a medical procedure where they take pictures of your insides in greater detail than an X-ray can provide. It is a time of great anxiety, with questions looming such as: Has the cancer returned? Or, even more for me, has the cancer grown? Some of the cancer had been left in me, by mutual decision, because of the high risk of organ loss or death via the scalpel. The cancer was in a very vital and complicated part of the human body around arteries and veins in the chest area. I had elected, with the encouragement of Dr. Wang, to leave the cancer in and hope the chemo had fully done its job. All the choices available to me involved high risks, but this seemed like the best choice of a motley set of options.

For Denel and I (we didn't tell the kids; they had spent too long in this valley with us already), it was like revisiting the valley of the shadow of death. We were again right in the middle of that very painful, turbulent season of our lives we had thought and hoped we were done with. I had no symptoms, but this didn't really provide the reassurance it might have since I hadn't had any symptoms with a seventeen-centimeter tumor in my abdomen either. I deeply hoped for good news, but despite her disagreement, I wanted to spare Denel from this part of the journey, especially if it was bad news. Thus, I went alone to meet with Dr. Wang after the scan to discuss the results.

My heart sank when he entered the office where I was waiting and quickly cut to the chase. He said there was bad news. The radiologist's report said there was growth in the cancer left behind on two sides, anterior and lateral. I was stunned. This could mean "here we go again"; this would mean even more severe chemo treatment or simply a death sentence since the area of cancer growth was, as I've said, inoperable. Displaying again his compassion and thoroughness, Dr. Wang had reviewed the CT scan films himself and said *he* couldn't detect any growth. He hoped the changes seen by the radiologist were scar tissue. Overall, this was very bad news with a layer of hope. After all, the radiologist is the expert at reading the films, not Dr. Wang.

The radiologist said growth on two sides. What now? I was in shock, an immobilized blob. Have you ever felt like the life has just been sucked right out of you? That's how I felt. Dr. Wang suggested we delay any treatment and redo the CT scan in three months.

I was fine with the possibility of three more months of life without chemo, but I also knew I needed to make some changes. I had kept all agreements I'd made with Denel about rest, diet, and work schedule. But if the cancer could grow in ideal circumstances, I had to again accept my limited control of things. What I could focus on was priorities at a higher level and having more urgency to get my affairs in order.

Telling Denel was painful for us both—hell revisited. Her questions were about why, and mine were about how—how to take care of my family, how to deal with the expected chemo treatments, etc. She chose to focus on Dr. Wang's interpretation of the scan. I ramped up my efforts to get clarity and energy into the priorities of my life. I let go of some things and invested more in others. Quick fruit and priorities of most importance ruled the day. After all, I didn't know how many days I had left. We did not tell the kids or anyone else. It would be painful for them and painful for us to tell. We shielded them and ourselves with the hope that Dr. Wang's reading of the scan was correct.

The next three months went quickly. Then it was time for the next CT scan. Denel would not leave my side this time, nor did I want her to. We would share this painful vulnerability together. The time for high anxiety was the meeting with Dr. Wang after the scan. We held our breath. If the cancer had continued to grow, I had very focused questions about chemo, quality of life, and how much time I had left. We weren't laughing when Dr. Wang walked into his office like we had the first time we'd met him. He wasted no time and, with a big smile, told us there was no change in the scan. This meant there was no growth and, hopefully, he had been correct in his reading that the "growth" seen by the radiologist on the first CT scan was indeed scar tissue, as Dr. Wang thought and we all hoped. We were greatly relieved. We could breathe again.

In revisiting this process, it was surely hell for us. But I can only imagine the struggles Dr. Wang and his staff also experience as they go through this process with so many people on a daily basis—telling some people they were likely going to live and others they were going to die. It would be easy and probably easier to function in this role if you simply cut off your emotions. Dr. Wang clearly did not, however, and it made the experience for us much more human and comforting. He was there with us.

Although family and friends might eventually be angry we didn't let them know about this trial we had been through, in retrospect, it felt like the right decision. It was too painful to tell others, especially if we weren't sure. We were protecting them and ourselves, but it was grueling, nonetheless. But despite the good news in the end, the increased level of vulnerability and the abject dependence on those three-month scans were increasingly driven home to me. I now saw and lived life in three-month segments. I guess this was my new reality and my version of one day at a time. Planning, choices, and spending time and money were now all framed within these three-month segments. Everything depended on the next scan. Eventually Dr. Wang extended this out to six-month scan cycles, with hopes of eventual freedom and "cure" status still out there somewhere.

Jerry Duprez

I have participated for many years now in a weekly men's Bible study group. The group has now evolved into a weekly breakfast meeting where we share life, laugh, and support each other. I guess with the ever advancing age and girth of the group, you could call it the Breakfast Chub. In any event, the guys are real and provide a safe environment to examine our lives and support each other. As with any group of guys, we sometimes get opinionated and verbally on the edge. Phrases like "have the balls to … oh, sorry, Jerry" (laughter) or "grow a pair" (reduced to the singular for me) are bandied about. I take no offense. It cracks me up too. After all, it's true and more experiences in humility for me!

I also use the group to "out myself" sometimes regarding some of the other post-treatment physical changes to my also aging body. Indeed, I'm not sure whether some of the changes I've experienced are cancer treatment or age-related. In any event, my hair has thinned out enough where I can now get sunburned on my scalp if I'm out in the sun too long. This is a new experience for me and not a particularly pleasant one either. I also have more gas, from both exit sites, than ever before. Denel even makes me keep a big box of matches by the bed. Hey, maybe that's where some of her libido has gone! But for me and most guys, the smell of sulfur is sexually stimulating … actually, *any* smell for guys is sexually stimulating! Regardless of cause, I am now more of an openly broken human than ever before. But I am still loving and still loved—all good. I guess I am forever changed but also forever grateful.

REDEMPTION FOR ONE, HEALING FOR MANY

As I conveyed in the introduction, the closer I got to my likely death, one of my greatest pains was realizing Denel would be burying her second husband. Her first husband, Ken Wrede, was a police officer for West Covina, California, a quiet suburb forty miles from Los Angeles. He was killed in the line of duty. This chapter chronicles that tragedy and the eventual recovery for Denel, Ken's parents, and three sisters.

Healing comes in many forms. I hope this book and this brief synopsis of the tragic loss of Ken provides some additional healing for her, his family, and his legacy as a West Covina police officer. You see, the circumstances leading up to his death resulted in a double violation, a double loss for him and his family. Responding to an apparent routine call of a man creating a disturbance in the neighborhood, he came upon a man who later was determined to be high on PCP. This is a drug that can at times create superhuman-like strength in people, often resulting in paranoia and aggression.

Ken was attempting to calm this individual down, assess the situation, and respond accordingly. Unfortunately, the individual initiated aggressive action toward Ken. A wrestling match ensued, and the suspect broke free, got into Ken's vehicle, and, with his bare hands, tore the shotgun out of the vehicle, metal bracket and all! Ken, in radio contact with his department, was apparently assured the weapon could not be fired while still in the bracket. Tragically, this was inaccurate. While still practicing restraint—the restraint we would all want and expect from those protecting us—he refrained from using his gun because lethal force was apparently not as yet necessary.

He displayed remarkable courage, but it cost him his life. The suspect, Michael Jackson, now on death row, somehow was able to fire the shotgun still in its holding bracket. Fragments pierced under Ken's left eye, and he apparently died quickly but not immediately. The first arriving officer witnessed his last throes of life before he took his final breath. Other arriving officers were eventually able to subdue the assailant with no further damage, but Ken, providing appropriate restraint in a quiet family neighborhood in suburban America, was dead. I will let Denel tell her own story from her experience, but you can imagine the pain in the tragedy. For her, they had been married only eleven months (their one-year anniversary wedding cake was still in the freezer), and for Ken's family, their twenty-six-year-old son, killed in the line of duty in a quiet American suburb, was too painful for words. Added salt in this wound was the fact that Ken was practicing appropriate and guided restraint that led to his sudden death.

What followed in the police community was shameful. Ken was branded somewhat as having ineffectively dealt with the situation. He wasn't viewed as forceful enough. Remember, he was told the shotgun could not be fired in its holding bracket. He had no right at that point to use lethal force. The information was wrong, and it cost him his life. I saw a client years later who was a police officer. He told me the circumstances around Ken's death were used for training purposes about what *not-to-do* for police officers in similar situations. Not only was the information about the bracket not included, but Ken was essentially blamed for his own death! The violation to his legacy was doubly painful for Denel and Ken's family.

Denel had every reason to sue the city. But many in the police community of West Covina were supportive in her healing process, and they were still seen as family. So despite the official stance that apparently was aimed at protecting the city from suit at the cost of Ken's legacy, she chose not to sue. She just wanted to heal and see justice for the assailant. Later, a new chief of police for West Covina, Frank Wills, actively sought a full healing for Denel and Ken's family. Ken's name was eventually cleared, and the honor long due him— not just for dying, but for serving bravely and well— was posthumously bestowed. A street was named after him (Wrede Way in West Covina), part of the I-10 freeway along a five-mile stretch in West Covina was memorialized to him, and Kenneth S. Wrede Memorial ceremonies were held in 2006. All of this in an appropriate attempt by Chief Wills to rectify some wrongs was long overdue but much appreciated. Hopefully any future police training pertaining to the events leading to Ken's death will tell the whole story, honoring his brave legacy.

Ken's parents, as part of their healing process, started an organization, COPS—Concerns of Police Survivors. Building an organization to serve a good cause was their own way to both give and bring healing to others and themselves. It was established in an effort to support and facilitate overcoming/recovery for the family members of fallen police officers. The experience of survivors is unique in each case, of course, but shares the senselessness of tragic, non-war death—in Ken's case, death protecting an otherwise safe, quiet American suburb. Although they can't bring back their son, Ken's parents, Marianne and Ken, found some valuable meaning and purpose and, for them, a path to overcoming their loss.

When our Nikki was in eighth grade and visiting Washington, DC, with her class, we accompanied her for part of that trip. Denel and I were able to visit the memorial to fallen police officers there. It was a moving experience for us both. For her, it was a comforting acknowledgement of her own individual tragedy. For me, it was an up close perspective of the pain I've shared with her secondarily. (Emotionally charged events like trial and retrial issues for Michael Jackson, anniversaries, and contacts with Ken's family, etc., August 31—the day Ken was killed—will never feel normal for her again.)

What Chief Wills helped to fully heal was Ken's legacy and Denel's relationship with Ken's entire family. There was no direct animosity between them, but the gravity of a tragedy like theirs has a way of bringing division. To continue in relationships essentially means continuing the intimate connection with painful loss. Grieving and recovery processes are uniquely individual. It's what often breaks up marriages when a child dies. Tragic loss can be, at least for a time, too painful on existing relationships to be borne. The last memorial for Ken put on through Chief Wills' efforts gave Denel and Ken's parents an opportunity to reconnect at a time when much healing had already taken place for them all. Ken was genuinely and appropriately being honored. It was a watershed moment for healing, not just for Denel and Ken's parents, but apparently for the entire West Covina Police Department and family.

I never met Ken, but I experienced Denel's pain each time with the aforementioned milestone events and with each siren she'd hear for years, each ambulance en route, each police car, each uniformed officer incidentally seen in the community—persistent and spontaneous reminders to her of her pain. The journey was wearying at times for me, and I was on the outside looking in. I couldn't go to retrials for Michael Jackson. I had a separate peace about that, but I understood her need to be there. She needed closure.

At Ken's freeway dedication ceremony in 2006, I was surprised at how much emotion came up in me. Even though I didn't know him personally, I felt like I got to know him through Denel over the years. Much more, however, was the pain I'd shared with Denel for over twenty years. Healing and closure for us all, and justice for Ken's legacy and how he would be remembered.

Beauty from Ashes: Denel's Story

When I met Jerry, Ken's death was still really fresh for me; the trial date for his killer was set, and I was attempting to rebuild my life. The very orderly life I had established was destroyed, my husband was dead, and I had a lingering sense the family wasn't being told the whole story. To compound matters, Ken's family and I were being discouraged from attending the trial! Although Michael Jackson, Ken's killer, was convicted of first-degree murder with special circumstances and given the death penalty, apparent justice for his crime, it never seemed that Ken was considered the hero we believed him to be.

I truly believe God, in His grace and love, brought Jerry and me together during a difficult time in both our lives. We were new therapists in a private practice in Alta Loma, California. We married in 1985; had our daughter, Nicole, in 1986; and launched our own practice—Haven Psychological Associates—in 1987. In addition, Jerry received his PhD in counseling psychology from USC the same year. Our lives were a whirlwind of activity, about which we felt very blessed. At the same time, I struggled to integrate such a sudden, violent loss with the forward motion of my life.

From the moment Michael Jackson, Ken's killer, was sentenced to death, a legal team vowed to utilize anything and everything to appeal it. In the ensuing years, there were numerous state and federal hearings on behalf of this career criminal and drug addict, allowing him to exercise his *rights* as an American. In the meantime, my family and Ken's family felt very little closure or sense of justice, instead feeling frustrated and re-victimized by a system that seems to favor the criminal.

Jerry and I had our son, Christopher, in 1990, and I worked part-time while Jerry worked full time in the practice, which is five miles from our home. As I strove to balance a home, children, and a career, I slowly healed, working through deep pain and loss. I knew true healing means integrating grief and woundedness into our lives—a truly difficult task—while living in the present and trusting God for the future.

As believers, God reassures us that "*all* things work together for good," even when we can't begin to imagine that truth (Romans 8:28, NIV). We are also encouraged to "trust in the Lord with all your heart, and lean not on your own understanding," which is so very difficult when we feel such a need to figure out *why* bad things happen and try to regain some sense of control over our lives (Proverbs 3:5, NIV). I knew God had blessed me with Jerry and our children, but the pain of *how* Ken died and the perception by the law enforcement community, that he lost his life due to his own reluctance to act or protect himself, haunted me. I could only trust that one day God would lead me to understanding.

In 2001, the Ninth Circuit Court of Appeals overturned Michael Jackson's death sentence, and in 2002, the penalty phase was retried. I was determined to attend and be involved with the trial, as were Ken's parents and two of his sisters, Karen and Kerry. We began meeting with Darren Levine, Deputy District Attorney for Los Angeles County Crimes Against Police Officers Division. This is when I began seeing God's hand. Darren was, and is, an amazing man and gifted prosecutor. He committed himself not only to securing another death penalty verdict but to restoring honor to Ken as well.

At that time, our family was attending Community Baptist Church in Alta Loma. I noticed a woman who looked familiar a number of times, and one Sunday we ended up seated next to one another. I racked my brain during the service and finally realized she had been an officer with Ken at West Covina Police Department who I hadn't seen in years. I asked if her name was Patti—she said yes but looked quite uncomfortable. She proceeded to tell me she had been afraid to say anything because she thought I might still be "mad" at her. I was incredulous and told her I had never been mad at her and asked her why she would think such a thing. That's when God began to give me the understanding I had been asking for. I was shocked when she told me that she had been instructed not to attend Ken's funeral because I didn't want her there—a flat-out lie! Many tears were shed, and healing began that day as I assured her I had always considered her a friend, and we began to piece together what really happened the day Ken was killed. In the months to follow, Patti, Karen, Joe, (one of Ken's closest friends and a cop), Darren Levine, and I began the quest to learn the truth and honor Ken's bravery and heroism.

As we pieced together what happened leading up to Ken's death, we learned that as he called for backup, a sergeant came on the radio and stated that the shotgun was inoperable in the rack. We had never been made aware of that. This fact was quite possibly the deciding factor in Ken *not* using lethal force. In fact, the officers on duty that day were so enraged at the sergeant for broadcasting that that some of them allegedly threatened to harm him. Patti began attempting to reach me to make me aware of what Ken had been told; however, she was then strongly urged "not to bother me" and was ordered by a lieutenant not to attend the funeral, supposedly at my request.

We speculated that the department's concern was liability. The information that was covered up only seemed to deepen the pain and further traumatized those of us who loved Ken by "blaming the victim."

As with so many things in life, I believe the retrial was a blessing in disguise. The need to revisit Ken's murder provided multiple opportunities for truth, healing, and reconciliation. Justice was upheld. Ken's honor, courage, and character were recognized, the family received support and appreciation, and Ken's legacy was restored.

Not only did a second jury sentence Michael Jackson to death, but the current police chief at West Covina Police Department, Frank Wills, has made it his personal mission to honor our family and bestow on Ken all the respect and gratitude he deserved. I am grateful to God that his legacy has been restored and God showed me He truly is the Great Redeemer!

> And provide for those who grieve in Zion-
> to bestow on them a crown of beauty
> instead of ashes,
> the oil of joy
> instead of mourning,
> and a garment of praise
> instead of a spirit of despair.
> They will be called oaks of righteousness,
> a planting of the Lord
> for the display of his splendor.

Isaiah 61:3 (NIV)

Jerry Duprez

OVERCOMING FOR US ALL

My conception of overcoming throughout my life has generally been about winning, achieving, and accomplishing something in direct opposition to the apparent obstacle in question. Sometimes those obstacles were external situations, events, or even people that presented a clear block to my chosen path. But probably more often the obstacles I've had to overcome have been internal ones: wounds, self-perceptions, or limitations that I created myself, either all by myself or as interpretations of life events. I think if we're honest with ourselves, this is true for most of us. The obstacles become ingrained in our thought process as automatic, assumed truth. Indeed, an entire school of psychotherapy (cognitive-behavioral) was created to systematically address this thought process. Although valuable, I think there are many thoughts, feelings, and wounds that get encapsulated in a poorly articulated state in the human spirit that go deeper and beyond the techniques involved in cognitive behavioral therapy.

The limits, assumptions and self-expectations that echo deep within in a whispered voice require, from my perspective, a combination of spiritual and psychological struggling to eventually overcome by surpassing and/or accepting and by finding meaning and purpose at the core of the experience. First in this process is awareness and then overcoming before we can move forward. By forward, I don't just mean what we currently strive for, who we want to be, but ultimately who God wants us to be. He sees us without the colored, stained glasses we look in the mirror through. Acceptance seems key here.

For me, I've now come to see overcoming as more than just winning, achieving, or even healing, but finding meaning and purpose in the process. If I die, so what? But if I live well and leave a legacy that's been worked out from the depths of my soul, great. Within my human limits, I've overcome death. I've done what I'm capable of, not by living forever (on this earth), but by holding on to a semblance of dignity and courage in the process. My trusting God, *no matter* what outcome He chooses, and leaving a legacy I can be at peace with for my loved ones, is what matters most. From a spiritual perspective, of course, only Jesus Christ overcame death, and that is a gift by grace to us. But I *can* overcome the meaninglessness that is often associated with life and death. I am capable of overcoming, and furthermore, I am arguably responsible to both myself, others, and God to do just that. Aren't you also?

The following brief narrative I wrote for my clients. I keep it in a holder outside my office door and give it to any who want it. It is meant to be an encouragement, as we are all clients in someway, with much to overcome. For my clients, I am honored and privileged to walk alongside them on their journey through life.

Since one entire wall and parts of two others in my office are painted as a replica of the Boston Red Sox stadium, Fenway Park, and its left field wall (the "Green Monster," it's called), a lot of clients will initially say, "Oh, I see you like baseball," or "I see you're a Red Sox fan." I explain that although I do like baseball, the Angels are actually my favorite team and there's so much more to the story. It is a story rooted in sports but one that speaks to the beauty of the human spirit in the journey to overcome. Invariably, my clients come into my office, needing to overcome something: anxiety, depression, brokenness of various kinds, addictions, broken marriages, or broken spirits. There is hope, meaning, and purpose in the process of healing. This process combines overcoming with acceptance, which leads to peace and freedom. My wish and my work are directed toward this goal for all my clients and readers.

The mural in my office is an artistic rendering of the left field wall at Boston's Fenway Park, baseball's famed "Green Monster." However, it is far more a tribute to the capacity of the human spirit to overcome than it is purely a baseball story. In 1919, after several World Series appearances and much success, the Boston Red Sox essentially sold possibly the greatest player of all time, Babe Ruth, "the Great Bambino," to the New York Yankees—a colossal mistake. The Yankees went on to register more championships than any sports franchise of any kind since that trade. The Red Sox went nearly seventy years before another World Series appearance, coming within one late-inning error of victory before losing the series to another New York team, the Mets. The fact that the man who committed the costly error was hobbled by injuries and had courageously overcome much to help his team get to the Series was lost on most. Failure was all that could be seen.

Then in 2004, in the American League Championship Series against their archrivals, the Yankees, the Red Sox were down three games to zero in a seven-game series. Never before in the history of baseball had a team come back from a 3–0 deficit to win a championship series and go on to the World Series, let alone against the mighty Yankees. The Red Sox had to overcome their own history and an impossible present obstacle. In late-inning dramatic fashion, the Red Sox won game four. Game five, represented in the mural, went fourteen innings before more dramatics by the Sox won it, sending the series back to New York for game six and, if necessary, game seven. The Red Sox won both those games too and went on to sweep the World Series for their first world championship in nearly a century.

This mural is not simply a tribute to a baseball team. All baseball fans and all those who have struggles to overcome in any area of their life can appreciate what the Red Sox accomplished. It represents a celebration of what each of us is capable of. We have all made mistakes—sometimes colossal, often repeated. We have all been wounded and met obstacles—some self-created, some natural, some generational—and at times perceived them as insurmountable. We *all* need to overcome. This mural is meant as an inspiration to each of us to write new scripts for our lives, to persevere through difficult times, even times that feel endless and overwhelming, as if those struggles are more than us. By using the power within, from others and above, we all can overcome. Thank you for the privilege of becoming one of your fans, and may God bless you in your own personal journey to overcome.

ETIOLOGY

Etiology is a medical and psychological term about causation. We all would like the illusion of control that comes with knowing that because we did this or that, we got cancer. The control comes in with stopping or adding those things to your life, and thus you can control whether you get (re-get) cancer. This is, in my opinion, a half truth. There is clear research evidence linking certain practices to increasing your risk of certain cancers (smoking, excessive sun exposure, diet, sedentary lifestyle, stress, etc.). There are also certain lifestyle practices that reduce but do not eliminate these risks (diet, exercise, marriage, believe it or not, etc.). It is a responsible and productive, albeit imperfect, way to live a healthy lifestyle to maximize the positive and minimize the negative parts of these risk factors.

But certainty is, again, unobtainable. Genetic, environmental, and numerous other factors all play a role in the development of cancer. What's more, doctors tell us that just about every man, if he lives long enough, will get prostate cancer. What a bummer, huh, guys? It just doesn't seem fair, if that is all there is. The human species is the only one that is aware of its own mortality.

We know we will all die eventually. It gives meaning, purpose, and direction to how we live—or at least it can.

As for me, I too wondered about my role in the causation of my cancer. Unlike my dear mother-in-law, Millie, I don't expect to find a definitive answer that I can then control and outlive Methuselah. But that doesn't relieve me of the responsibility to look in the mirror. What I found was both not surprising and enlightening. I have what clinicians call obsessive-compulsive tendencies. I worry, control, work hard, need closure, am productive, and worry and worry—did I say worry? I wanted to make sure I included that. I also have trouble letting go. This is the type of personality that gets things done and accomplishes much in a lifetime. It produces doctors and achievers, but joy, process, and relationships sometimes suffer. It is hard on the individual *and* those around them. The spiritual equivalent would be the Martha lifestyle. It is a focus on the tasks, duties, and responsibilities while the bigger picture sometimes gets lost. The biblical story of the sisters Mary and Martha is a good example here. Jesus was visiting the sisters and their brother, Lazarus. This, of course, was a very special honor and time for the sisters. Mary was entranced with the presence of Jesus and sat at His feet, listening to His every word. Martha was busily engaged in the work of preparing the meal and readying the house for their special guest. Martha soon became resentful of her sister's lack of help and told Jesus to essentially make her lazy sister help her. Jesus's reply was that Mary was doing the better thing and He wouldn't take that from her. It's not that responsibilities, tasks, and work don't have their place. They absolutely do. It's just that the obsessive-compulsive/Martha style does not discern well when this style fits the situation and when it does not.

The compulsion to do sometimes gets us—make that me—lost in minutia that are not nearly as important as the bigger picture. I have lived my life like Martha. Although I have accomplished much and, to my credit, richly touched many people, I had developed a pretty resentment-based lifestyle. This is what this style can lead to, doing all the right things without joy, happiness, or a sense of enough appreciation from others. This was the surprising revelation for me. Until I began to look at my resentments, I hadn't realized how deep and pervasive they were. I literally could develop ten or more resentful feelings/statements on my five-mile drive to work! From the guy going too slow, to the guy going too fast, to the guy who didn't signal—you get the picture. The resentments came like a flood, and if they came that much on a simple five-mile drive, what about the other areas? I came to realize that I was, and largely still am, a judgmental, unforgiving, resentment-filled individual. Did this cause or even have an impact on my development of cancer? I don't know. But what was clear is that it is a toxic lifestyle. I had to change that regardless of its impact on my cancer. I just didn't want to live that way. It made me sick to look at it.

As I set about to change this (I've only just begun; thank you, Carpenters), I realized I needed a prayerful process that included people who I could legitimately say had wronged me. It didn't matter; I had to let go, and that was very hard for me. As I started including the "wrongdoers" in my prayers, I asked God for blessings on them and to help me release my resentments. Unfortunately, the list kept growing, so now I have to get up a little earlier each morning to go through my prayers! I am nowhere near done with this process, but I feel freer. I am carrying much less these days. I in no way have this down, but when I see a driver going too fast (in my not-so-humble opinion), I try to remember to bless them since they must be in a hurry for a good reason. Of course, I do this right *after* I get irritated and resentful; let's not change overnight, okay? Forgiving the "wrongdoers" in our lives is probably the hardest *and* most freeing process. Christians are called to love their enemies. This is not a theoretical command. It is actual, practical, and very hard to genuinely do. It is the highest road. God has his reasons for this, many of which we can't know but maybe some of the benefit is the health we get both physically, psychologically, and, most especially, spiritually. I have to let go. I will, eventually, when they stop messing with me, when they learn how wrong they are, after God smites them—no, I just have to let go, maybe you too. We have all been wronged, *and* we have all wronged others.

As I close, I hope this little book has touched you and yours. If it has in any way helped you, please pass that blessing on to others. It will make both my pain and yours all the more meaningful and valuable. May God bless you always and in all ways!

Consider it pure joy, my brothers, whenever you face trials of many kinds because you know that the testing of your faith develops perseverance ...

James 1:2

And perseverance, character, and character, hope and hope does not disappoint us.

Romans 5:4–5

... And death has been swallowed up in victory.

1 Corinthians 15:54

... Our Savior, Jesus Christ, who has destroyed death.

2 Timothy 1:10

And free those who all their lives were held in slavery by their fear of death.

Hebrews 2:15

CELEBRATION

This last chapter is essentially, on paper, what I envision(ed) for my memorial service. During the treatment of my cancer, this was a lot more necessary a thing to think about, but as part of my legacy, I am glad that it has been created. This is not meant to be a morbid sentiment; rather, an example to consider when mapping out your own legacy. These are words deep from within my heart, whether my own personal words or song lyrics that I deeply connect with when thinking about my love for family and friends. I want all of this to be conveyed in the context of celebration and joy for the love and life in my years on earth. As I said previously, I recorded my voice reading what follows:

I thank you all for coming today. You wouldn't be here if I didn't love you. Although this celebration—and it is meant to be a celebration of our relationships—is, like me, kind of weird, it will hopefully be a joyful acknowledgement of all you have meant to me, how much I have loved you all, and how blessed I have been to have you in my life. People will sometimes say that struggles have become blessings; I've experienced that at times in my life, but mostly that seemed out of my faithful reach. But with this illness, the growth and time with my kids and grandkids, and the loving support from so many family, friends, and clients, I've had to learn how to receive through all this. I can honestly say, despite my passing, that this has been a blessing. I have felt deeply loved. I am, as you all know, a deep, complicated, loving cornball. We went on a family cruise once, and the cruise staff would give cheap little nothing-type gifts, and the audience would collectively say, in unison, "Ooh, aah, so what." This next part is an audience-participation exercise. Please repeat that phrase with each pause. I have accomplished many things in my life:

> I graduated with a double major in philosophy and PE from APC..."Ooh, aah, so what";
> I got two masters degrees from CSLA: special ed and psych;
> I got my PhD from USC;
> I consulted and authored many programs in mental health facilities;
> I was a partner with HPA;
> I have loved God and all of you as best I could and with all my heart—that is the only thing that really matters...(no "ooh, ah" to that)

To Denel: For quite a while, I had a hard time reconciling a loving God with the notion that He would allow you to bury your second husband or Belinda to be an orphan in her thirties or Gabe and Angel to bury their second dad and me to miss Nikki's wedding. But then I realized that I have loved you, Lup, from the bottom of my heart and soul for a quarter century. How blessed we have both been by that time and love. And Belinda, although your parents may have been slow to love you in mature ways, your mom and I truly have loved you. We've overcome much, and despite how inadequately I may have filled Armando's shoes, I have loved you, Gabe and Angel, as a father, and that is good. I hope it makes a difference in your lives. I have lived my life in the hope that Jesus would greet me one day and say to me, little old me, "Well done, my good and faithful servant." I hope your dad will say to me, "Well done, my good and faithful friend." Know, my Nikki, that I will be at your wedding in spirit, probably with a corny joke, but I have and always will cherish you. Denel, I not only give you permission, but I implore you to be happy, enjoy family, and friends, drink wine, and yuck it up with Millie, Denise, and Nikki. If you want to risk loving again, you deserve nothing but the best, my Dulcinea del Toboso, my caramia, my Luper, my soulmate. You've told me many times that I am your hero. Those words, especially after nearly twenty-five years of marriage, have meant the world to me, but through all the illness and struggles, you've taken care of me better than I thought you could. I'm sorry for underestimating your great strength; *you* are my hero!

To Belinda: You are my firstborn. I learned to love children through you. From scaring you with my Santa imitation, letting you drive the VW across the dirt at APC when you were three, to the fine young woman you've become today. You have always been deep in my heart. We've overcome much, and we'll overcome this too, for I will always be with you. Oh, that's a scary thought, huh? I love you with all my heart, Jelinda Bean Pudray! The time we've had recently has been special to me beyond words, and I am blessed because I did get to be a part of your wedding and having children. Being a bigger part of the boys and girls' lives has been great. They are fine children, and you've done a fine job with them…

To my Nikki: Beanie, Bean Beauty, Dollie, Niconole, financial black hole, Nikki my Nikki, Missy Lee, Bee-Sting Lips (Uncle Bill). This will be a little longer, not because I love you more, but because there were so many things I was waiting to say at your wedding I'll have to say them now. You are, like your mother, 85 percent absolute gift from God and 15 percent "Whoa, Nellie!" Any man you call husband will have to learn to love that 15 percent too because it, although wearisome at times, is also a wonderful gift from God, just like I learned with your mom. I have some stories I need to tell. When you and Chris were about eight and four respectively, you had the coolest Barbie battery-powered Corvette—the cat's meow. Then we got Chris a little jeep. Being only four, it took him a while to learn how to drive it, but it had two speeds; yours only had one. Driving them side-by-side in the street one day, he shifted into second gear and passed you. When you realized you couldn't keep up, you stopped, opened the door, got out, left the car there, and never drove it again. Very intense, you were—that's our Nikki. Your mom and I used to say that, like her, you were so competent and independent that you could have gladly had your own apartment at twelve years old, and I'm sure many times you wish you had! When you first started to drive, I was petrified with your first accident, very scared with the second, etc., until I was just utterly amazed with the sixth that the Jetta was still okay! That car had so many different parts in it, it had identity issues! Although it scared me greatly when you had your appendectomy, I got to spend so much time with you because you had to slow down—that was special for me. I helped you write a term paper and finally redeemed myself with an "A" opposed to the "B" I received when I helped you in high school, which was an added bonus of our time together. I saved a little face anyway. You have always had your own mind and your own heart, and they are wonderful. I adore you. I even love your names for me: "Papa" and "Daddy" when I said "yes," "Caca" when I said "no," and "Big Booty," when I gained weight. Some man you call husband one day will be very lucky, and he better be on the ball!

To Chris: Christopher Dillon, Tuffy, Tuffy the Rubber-Nosed Goofball. You have the heart of a lion, my son. It has caused you and us problems at times, but it is good. It is from God, and it has been a deep blessing to see you grow in the use of that big heart and strong will. I am very proud of you. You have overcome much and have been a joy and inspiration to your mom and me. When I told you about the cancer up in Pismo Beach, you said, "It can't be, Dad; you're superman. You can't be sick." I have dedicated myself to loving you and others in a way I hoped you would emulate. You are becoming that person. You will be different than me;

your mom and I gave you a healthier sense of ownership of your power than we had, but you will be better than me. That is the hope of every father for their sons. You too, Gabe. I also told you up in Pismo that there were greater losses than yours and I needed you to step up, consider deeply the needs of others, and whenever best put those needs before your own. You are learning to do that, and that is such a blessing to your mom and me. We have had more time together than most fathers and sons ever get: Coaching and cheering for you in sports, "the Chris." Playing, watching movies together on the couch (*Hook* forty times, *The Sandlot* thirty-five times, *Home Alone* fifteen times, *Surf Ninjas* ten times, etc.). How you roped me into joining Tae Kwon Do ("Dad, if I get to blue belt, will you join?" Forty-plus-year-old hips just don't rotate outward.) to the week we spent in the hotel preparing for your black belt test. I remember that day in the pool when you suddenly realized that "short man" was a better description for me than you. You couldn't stop laughing at the realization that you had outgrown me. I thought you were going to split a gut. I also loved all of our trips to Der Weinerschnitzel—sorry again for not catching the bad dog you ate at the Quakes game. We have been blessed, son. Take what's best of that little Italian woman and me and use that great heart and strength to make this a better world. I am better for having you as a son!

Gabe: Gabriel Armando Favela, Gabby Man. In the tradition of your dad, I have tried to support, teach, model, and love you. However inadequately I've done it, I've tried to be a father for you that was always going to be second-best, but know that I have done my best to love you as a father. Your dad is in you, and hopefully I've put some gifts in there too. If you are going to honor the gifts your dad and I have given you, you will continue to grow in cherishing and taking care of Angel and your mom and someday give some of those gifts back to your own children and hopefully others as well. I love you, Gabby Man. Pass it on.

Angel: Angelita. I have loved you no less than Gabe, but there didn't seem to be as many opportunities to show it over the years. You still had your mom, and you also had your uncle Dan, but know that you are loved. And on your wedding day, your dad and I will be there supporting you, whoever walks you down the aisle, and ready to wreak havoc on your hubby if he ever mistreats you! You have what Belinda and Nicole have: a very sweet, rich heart and a whole lot of inner strength. It will serve you well. Go Angelize the world!

Don: Brothers are loved, but you have been that rare blessing that defies the usual. You are my brother *and* my best friend. I have three best friends; I have been truly blessed. You have believed in me in ways that helped me to see past family of origin limitations, to see the bigger picture and my place in it. I can't thank you or love you enough. You are a rock. I hope Chris and Gabe will keep learning from you in how to live life, be a man, and love others. I know I have. I love ya, Don, you are truly the Duke of Big!

Billy and John: I can't separate you two knuckleheads. To have three best friends, to have friends—really brothers—like you two for over thirty-five years has been an unbelievable blessing to me. From forehead jokes (Bill), nose jokes (John), and my racial heritage, nothing was sacred, off-limits, or approached without humor or love. Through good times and bad, we've cried a little, laughed a lot, and loved always—a good model for how to live life. Please continue to touch the lives of my—make that our—family with your wisdom, strength, and compassion. You have made my life so much better for having shared it with me. I thank you and God for you two. Now promise me that for the rest of your lives you will *not* have a good time without me!

Mike: Mikey, Miguel Pablito. We have shared much through Naynay, divorce, and distance. Know that whatever obstacles kept us from more time together over the past years I have always loved you and felt loved by you. Your truckload of cards and ever-present availability during my illness has been a deep blessing, which is much appreciated, and has brought tears to my eyes on several occasions. Thank you for you, and thank you for that rescue after the divorce at APU. I love you, Mikey!

Tom: You play the distant hard-ass well, but it's all smoke. You are a deeply loving, very funny, enigma of human matter. I have always felt very loved by you. From the recurring comedy tapes when I was down, to doing such a great job taking care of Dad (and us), to your feeble but valiant efforts at overcoming your "Fullerton Tom/Snohomish Tom" travel limitations, you have too been an odd but wonderful blessing to me. I love ya, Tommy. Now get a life and visit Don and Mike!

Eddie and Millie: You have accepted me into your family from the beginning with loving arms. You have been like parents to me. That was painful at first, as I think you can understand with my mom and dad gone, but you never judged, just waited and loved me as much as I would let you. Eddie, you were supposed to be dead twenty years ago and were perfectly willing to go. It ticks me off a little that I'm gone and you are still hanging around! Seriously, you have been a wonderful patriarch of this family, a tradition I have sought to emulate. I hope I have done a good job and you can say, "Well done, my good and faithful son-in-law." Millie, Millitoia, Millicent June, the "Beep" Lady, you are the picture of grace, strength, and love combined. From your deep compassion, untiring sacrifices, and ever-present empathy, you have been a pillar that Denel and I have relied on for decades in raising the kids and raising ourselves. You are wonderful and you are loved. Any grandma that would take swimming lessons in her sixties so her grandkids could have a pool—a condition Safety Captain Jerry insisted on—is a person of unique strength and heart. I hope you keep "beeping" your way to one hundred years old. You are a blessing to me and all those around you.

Brian: I have always liked and loved you, Bri. I hope you know that deep in your heart despite our different views on what the family needs from you. I respect so many things about you: your intelligence, your heart, your character, your work ethic, your frugality, the way you've cared for your parents, your professional and educational accomplishments (no "ooh, ah, so what" for you!), and your overall strength and ability to overcome. I hope you continue to grow in the direction of a patriarch in the tradition of your dad and, to a lesser degree, me. I love ya, Bri Dog!

Grandkids: Joshua Ryan Isch: Joshy, I love you and wish you an inner voice that tells you over and over again, despite mishaps, what a gifted, good, and special person you are and that you choose only relationships that value you accordingly…

Korey: I love you, Kor, and wish you a path that is consistent with your gentle spirit and fulfills you in every way.

McKenna: You are too young, sweetheart, to know how special you are and how much you are loved, but I have no doubt that you are going to tackle that world out there!

Cassidy: Cass, Cassadoodle, Cassidy Bodacity, your endless, rambling, monologue telephone calls to Grandma and me have been a unique and special blessing, just like you are. I love you.

Friends: I'm not going to single anyone out. What we've meant to each other is in the nature of our relationship, and I've been blessed with too many of you. You'd all be asleep before I got done. Please know that you have enriched my life and my passing immeasurably, and I love you for that. Enjoy the music, the day, and each other. I am thanking God for you all!

Music

Me:

"Desperado" (Eagles)
"Dr. My Eyes" (Jackson Brown)
"I Wish It Would Rain" (Temptations)
"Your Love, Oh Lord" (Third Day)
"Darkness, Darkness" (Youngbloods)
"I Can't Take the Pain" (Third Day)
"Mercy" (Jake Hamilton)
"Just Call My Name" (Third Day)
"I Feel Like I'm Born Again" (Third Day)

For My Dulcinea Del Toboso, My Caramia, My Luper:

"Heaven Must Have Sent You" (Marvin Gaye and Tammy Terrell)
"Broken Road" (Rascal Flatts)
"Color My World" (Chicago)
"Love Song" (Loggins and Messina)
"Loving You Too Long" (Otis Redding)
"Just You and Me" (Chicago)
"Tupelo Honey" (Van Morrison)
"You're Still the One" (Orleans)
"Run River Run" (Loggins and Messina)
"There You Are" (Rascal Flatts)
"That's the Way She Feels About You" (Youngbloods)
"Ain't Nothing Like the Real Thing" (Marvin Gaye and Tammy Terrell)
"I've Been Searching So Long" (Chicago)

"Ain't Too Proud to Beg" (Temptations)
"You're All I Need" (Marvin Gaye and Tammy Terrell)
"Crazy Love" (Van Morrison)
"You're My Everything" (Temptations)
"I'll Be There" (Jackson Five)

For Belinda:

"You're So Beautiful" (Youngbloods)

For Belinda, Denel, Nik, and Angel:

"Brown-Eyed Girl" (Van Morrison)

For Nikki:

"Butterfly Kisses/Daddy's Little Girl" (Bob Carlisle)
"I Loved You First" (Heartland)
"Travelin' Blues" (Loggins & Messina)

For Chris:

"There Will Be a Day" (Jeremy Camp)
"Just the Two of Us" (Will Smith)
"Simple Man" (Lynyrd Skynyrd)
"Finally Make It Home" (MercyMe)

For all my children and grandchildren:

"My Wish for You" (Rascal Flatts)

For my mom:

> "I'm Going Home" (Hootie and the Blowfish)
> "The Sound of Music" (Julie Andrews)
> "Summertime" (Porgy & Bess)

For my dad:

> "Leader of the Band" (Dan Fogleberg)
> "Storm Warning" (Bonnie Raitt)

For Eddie:

> "Amore" (Dean Martin)

For Millie:

> "Evergreen" (Barbra Streisand)

For all my friends and family:

> "Shower the People You Love With Love"
> (James Taylor)
> "Ain't No Mountain High Enough" (Diana Ross
> and the Supremes)
> "Higher Ground" (Van Morrison)
> "You've Got a Friend" (James Taylor)
> "Free Bird" (Lynyrd Skynyrd)
> "I Just Want to Praise You" (Mary Mary)
> "Stay" (Jackson Brown)
> "Welcome Me Home" (Kenny Loggins)/Release
> balloons together during song.

APPENDIX A

To: Kaiser Permanente/Whom It May Concern,

My wife and I are in the healing profession (LCSW and PhD). As such, we fully appreciate the need to combine compassion and skill as we work with people. In our field (psychology), it's probably more art than science, but regardless, the two have to be combined to be effective. This letter is a commendation of several doctors and nurses in the Kaiser system who went above and beyond in combining the science and art of healing care to restore my health and in dealing with my wife and I as *people*, not just patients.

Dr. Delo, as my primary care physician, has always been responsive, flexible, and thorough in this role toward me. We thank him. Dr. Marnoy was able to diagnose my celiac disease in nine fewer years than the American average. Furthermore, his thoroughness resulted in the detection of my stage 3 testicular cancer despite the absence of symptoms. We thank him. Dr. Wang, from beginning to end, was honest, open, compassionate, and responsive to our needs. Indeed, he celebrated our victory of recovery fully with us. He extended himself on several occasions with phone calls, information, and options that were tremendously helpful in our securing the necessary planning to facilitate maximum family and church support. We thank him. Overall, together with exceptionally gentle and compassionate nursing care in the oncology/chemotherapy department (especially Terry, Lupe, MaLou, and Maria—we thank them), we couldn't be more pleased with the quality of people and professional care we received from Kaiser.

I can now resume my career as a psychologist. I hope I will be even more equipped to meet the needs of those clients I serve from my experience as a patient with your organization. My wife, my family, and I deeply appreciate the care we received from your organization.

Sincerely,

Gerald R. Duprez, PhD

APPENDIX B

He Has the Heart of a Rhinoceros

By: Doug Buche, 2010

He lost one part and lost his hair.
It grew back, at least his hair did,
Even better than it was before.

He kept his heart, but it got bigger,
As if to make up for the part he lost.
He kept on track; he kept his bearings.
The man had the heart of a rhinoceros.

Now that's an animal of great proportion.
Its horny hairdo grows straight out of his head.
A horn aphrodisiacal, mystical, considered spiritual,
It has been said.

Its armor coat more metallic than like skin, still sensitive to
The smallest flea, covers a tank-like body which should not
Move quickly, but still it does and with great force and with
great speed.

To compare a man to such a creature must seem
Preposterous. But not this man with a missing part.
Not like more of us, like the rhinoceros, he has its heart.

*Dedicated to my partner, Gerald Duprez

Jerry Duprez

APPENDIX C

This is a prayer I said every day during my treatment for cancer. It helped me along the path of surrender and in keeping my eyes lifted. It was key in staying focused and afloat. I chose to share it with you because it was instrumental in my overcoming, and I recommend that you adopt your own mantra as a means for coping and carrying on.

"Please take my burdens, Lord, and grow my joy and faith that the path I'm on is Your will for my life, that it honors You and that there will be fruit worthy of You and enough to sustain me. Please align me with my proper position with Denel and Flipside Church and children, and please grant me the peace that surpasses all understanding so that I may joyfully walk this path and finish the race You've set before me so that one day You may say to me in heaven, "Well done, my good and faithful servant."

APPENDIX D

My name is Nicole, and I am Jerry's daughter. I have had the privilege of helping my dad in the process of getting this book out to the world and the even greater privilege of being his daughter for the last twenty-four years.

Throughout the book, he mentions the topic of "God's will" a few different times. Like him, I used to believe that the infamous term had little to do with the bigger picture and matters of God's heart and completely with me: where I live, what I "do" with my life, etc. Don't get me wrong; I still believe God is very much involved and concerned with me and all the details of my life. It's just that I've had my world rocked in the last year, which has resulted in a broadening of my perspective and my understanding of what God's will *really* is for my life. God's will for my life, and for mankind in general, has so much more to do with holiness than it does vocation, location, or any other (no-)tion. God's will for my life is essentially and simply this: to love Him and to love people. To simplify things even more, loving people *is* loving Him. So really, God's will is for me to love people as a reflection of my relationship with Him, that His love would flow through me toward others. Again, I'm not saying that

God isn't fully capable and currently involved with the opening and closing of opportunity's doors and leading us in the "right" direction based on his design for us; I'm just saying these things take a backseat to His purpose for our lives.

These might seem like my own random thoughts that, merit or no merit, don't exactly have their place in Daddio's book. I chose to include this—asked to include, rather—because I wanted my dad and all of you to know that while he doesn't feel like he's ever been "good at discerning God's will," to the contrary, he has truly and richly lived a life of love. Anyone who has known him could attest to this. I wanted him to know that even if he's stuck on trying to figure out the mystery of life as if it's some treasure map that only God has the key to, like many of us get caught up in, he actually has a lot more figured out than most of us when it comes to God's heart and what He wills for our lives.

LEGACY WORKBOOK

Proverbs 13:22 "A good man leaves an inheritance for his children's children."

Diagnosis: A Life Shattered:

Diagnosis of a serious medical condition is a wake-up call, big time. It tends to severely puncture the denial we all generally live with regarding personal mortality. The following questions are meant to transition your awareness in this direction, but unfortunately, this process isn't necessarily gentle. Please remember that the overall benefit, the true gift of this awareness is the orientation it can provide toward cherishing all the blessings of this life and the push to live more urgently and authentically with our deepest values *today* with much enrichment in the living process for you and your loved ones.

If this workbook is being completed in a group format, share your initial self-ratings on the preparation scale.

1. We are all going to die someday. This means that I, _____,
   (your name here)
   am going to die someday. If I am both realistic and responsible, that means I need a will/trust and clear instructions and protection for my loved ones. In addition, for me personally, preparation steps I need to take are:

   _____

   _____

   _____

   _____

2. To enrich my life now and for as long as I live, I need to:

   _____

   _____

   _____

   _____

3. The changes I want to make are:

_____

_____

_____

_____

4. The priorities in my life need to be:

_____

_____

_____

_____

The Tower of Babel:

Remember, the whole point of these questions is to focus your life toward *living* in accord with your values, not about dying. If the questions become too difficult, please stop and/or get whatever professional or personal support you need. Also, don't forget the option of reading the narrative completely through first if that fits your needs better.

1. If I were diagnosed with a major illness/condition, my reaction would be:

_____

_____

_____

_____

2. I would eventually want to respond:

_____

_____

_____

_____

3. The issues it would bring up, the things I would need to take care of would be:

_____

_____

_____

_____

4. How important is it to your family that you live a long life?

_____

_____

_____

_____

5. What would you be willing to do to live a long life?

_____

_____

_____

_____

6. What do you need to change in your life to move toward a healthier lifestyle now?

_____

_____

_____

_____

Chemotherapy: The Wonderful Horror:

The nature of support and the nature of gifts/blessings have a uniquely personal quality to them as experienced by any individual. What *I* need, what I consider supportive isn't necessarily what you need or what you want as support from others. And blessings require both a personal perspective and a perspective in time. Perceiving cancer as a blessing either requires a degree of insanity (on my part!) or a long enough ride within the storm to see the benefits of calamity. Again, I am glad I didn't die (yet),but I came to appreciate the cancer as a blessing *before* I knew I would live. I had eight months of difficult but cherished living that gave me opportunities to clarify and communicate my love for others in a very rich way. Death enriches life if you let it.

1. If you were ill, what kind of support would be most helpful to you from family and friends?

_____

_____

_____

_____

2. How might a major illness be helpful to me, be a gift, in changing my life?

_____

_____

_____

_____

3. The things I'm most afraid of if I get a major illness or about death are:

_____

_____

_____

_____

Five Punches:

We have all probably felt and, realistically, been abandoned by someone in our lives. Unfortunately, if there are patterns to these experiences, we tend to expect the same in our relationship with God. He, however, operates on a different paradigm. No matter how low we may go or how convinced we are that He's checked out, time and perspective guide us to a new understanding.

1. When have you felt abandoned by God or totally alone and helpless?

_____

_____

_____

_____

2. What ultimately came to be your understanding of those times?

_____

_____

_____

_____

3. Who or what carried you when you felt that way?

_____

_____

_____

_____

4. Can you imagine or have you experienced such times as blessings/helpful in your life?

_____

_____

_____

_____

5. What would be the most difficult things to deal with for you if you had a major illness?

_____

_____

_____

_____

6. What are you most prideful about in your life?

_____

_____

_____

_____

7. How would you cope if you lost those things?

_____

_____

_____

_____

Learning to Receive:

Good, responsible people—Christian or not—often find it easier to give than to receive. Whether this is wonderful character structure, benevolence in action, a true following of Christ, or a not-so-altruistic need for control is somewhat of a moot point when the need to receive, or to be taken care of, becomes necessary. In essence, it involves your ability to be loved and maybe your belief in your lovability. When a major illness or other life event dictates the need, however, some people have no problem and allow others to love and take care of them. Some ultra-responsible Christians, being especially vulnerable in this area, have a very hard time reversing usual caretaker roles and embracing their own neediness. That was me, and I'm sure others might struggle here as well. I say that responsible Christians might be especially prone to this dilemma because Christians (and others, hopefully) are guided by the biblical golden rule of the standard to love others as we love ourselves. For the vast majority of people, this will mean that the spiritual imperative is to love others better than they are currently because loving themselves comes easily. For some, however, following this spiritual principle means we need to love *ourselves* better than we historically have if we are going to truly follow the guideline. For a significant minority of people, the conflict is more in loving themselves than others. Stepping up means allowing others to love us and to do as good a job with our own self care as we do taking care of others.

1. Is it easier for you to give or receive?

    _____

2. Do you have a sense of why that is?

    _____

    _____

    _____

    _____

3. Do you allow others to take care of you?

    _____

    How?

    _____

    _____

4. If you were to fully follow the golden rule, what changes would you need to make in your life?

Faith:

Faith is a hard thing to define, at least for me. As a noun, it is generic for religious/spiritual belief. As a verb, it is the engine—the computer processor, if you will—that drives, activates, and operates all the beliefs, all the programs of our lives. It is the real world expression of our inner being, our soul. It is the picture each of us paints that reveals ourselves. It is often the only thing those outside of our inner circle will ever see or know about our deepest beliefs. What picture do you paint to strangers? For me, it's probably akin to a Picasso: beautiful at times and in ways odd, disjointed, and double-minded. There are absolutes in the Christian faith, but they are centered on Christ, not politics, economics, or other worldly concerns.

Here the relevant question becomes what we project, what we paint for the world. Is it dominated by love or rules? To communicate, to *live* Christianity dominated by love and with rules, even absolute rules, is the challenge for every Christian. James addresses the issue of faith and its expression very concretely: "... Faith by itself, if it is not accompanied by action, is dead ... and ... I will show you my faith by what I do" (James 2:17, NIV). Clearly, for James, faith and action are inseparable. Hebrews 11:1 (NIV) offers us some further clarity: "Faith is being sure of what we hope for and certain of what we do not see." This describes a position we should take toward the multitude of uncertainties in life: having faith and trust. Faith grants peace where peace does not, maybe even should not, otherwise exist. But peace is individually defined. I had faith that God was in control, after many doubts and struggles, during the whole cancer ordeal, not faith in a particular outcome. Nikki, my daughter, had faith in a particular outcome, namely that I would survive. We both had peace and even the peace we each needed. But was her faith deeper, better, more mature than mine because it was specific? I don't know; what do you think? Regardless, we are all responsible, by God and/or our consciences, for the picture we paint in this world. The challenge for Christians is that ultimately this would be a loving work of art.

"... The only thing that counts is faith expressing itself through love."

Galatians 5:6 (NIV)

1. What do you most deeply believe in?

   _____

   _____

   _____

   _____

2. How do those beliefs affect significant struggles in your life?

   _____

   _____

   _____

   _____

3. Do you think any of the above would change for you if you had a major illness?

   _____

   _____

   _____

   _____

4. How would you define faith?

_____

_____

_____

_____

Sex:

There are many stigmas and myths about sex. One is
that to be a true man, I have to own and use my balls
("testicles," for you more sophisticated souls) to express
myself in the world. They somehow reflect power, control, and manhood. If I'm not using and expressing
myself through my balls, I am somehow less of a man.
How true do you think this is? How does society in
general reflect this concept?

1. What near-and-dear vital areas might a major
   illness affect in your life?

_____

_____

_____

_____

2. What are the most important things in your life?

_____

_____

_____

_____

3. How might a major illness change how you live?

_____

_____

_____

_____

4. Who and/or what would you lean on for support if a major negative (or positive can be stressful also) event occurred in your life?

_____

_____

_____

_____

Jerry Duprez

"Minor Surgery":

"Minor" is truly in the eye of the beholder. Recovery is necessary for us all because we are all broken. What each of us needs to recover from might be different and it is important we don't judge or assume someone else's mountain to climb is easier or less vital than our own. What is "major" to me might be "minor" to you and vice versa. We all could use a hand up the mountain trail. I know I still do.

1. What kind of support do you want in major life struggles?

   _____

   _____

   _____

   _____

2. What kind of support do you need?

   _____

   _____

   _____

   _____

3. What kinds of things do you need to recover from now in your life?

_____

_____

_____

_____

4. How might you begin that process?

_____

_____

_____

_____

5. Who might be a mentor, helper, and/or fellow trailblazer with you?

_____

_____

_____

_____

Jerry Duprez

Saying Good-bye:

Think back on the hardest thing you have ever done emotionally. Did you do it alone? How might you approach that same mountain today? Would you do it alone? I hope not. There is a strength in shared struggle. I have heard couples say over and over again that some of their very best, most connected years of marriage were the first few when they struggled the most. They had no money, more kids than hands, more problems than solutions, more work and stress than rest, but they were one in the struggle. I hope you find that wisdom and blessing in all your struggles.

1. If you were facing death in the immediate future, what would you feel the need to do?

2. If the things in question one are good/desirable things, what is stopping you from doing them now?

_____

_____

3. What can give you a sense of urgency to live more fully now?

_____

_____

_____

_____

4. Who would you lean on?

_____

_____

_____

_____

Major Surgery:

Remember a time or times when you were blessed in ways that made no sense, were beyond your expectations, and beyond anything you felt you deserved. Share those experiences with someone else today and pray for the same for someone else, today.

1. What have you learned from your hardest struggles in life?

_____

_____

_____

_____

2. How can you apply those lessons more fully in your life today?

_____

_____

_____

_____

3. Who or what can help you in that process?

_____

_____

_____

_____

4. Is there someone now in your life that you would especially want a great thing/blessing/miracle to happen for? Is there anything you can do to help make that happen? If there is, develop some plan and share it with someone … and do it.

_____

_____

_____

_____

Recovery Miracle:

Count your blessings. It is both a great phrase and a misnomer. A truly grateful spirit knows that our blessings are infinite but a good exercise anyway.

1. Have you ever literally written down all the things you are grateful for, the blessings in your life?

Yes   No

2. Write them down here (or somewhere) …

_____

_____

_____

_____

_____

_____

_____

_____

_____

3. Share them with someone…

4. Maintain the list and add to it daily…

Recovery Process:

Living with the Blessings of Limits:

A valid and healthy position in life is to assume responsibility for what we can control and live accordingly. Unfortunately, control is often an illusion and can result in pathological intensity that robs the very life out of things, especially relationships. The wisdom of the serenity prayer from Alcoholics Anonymous is relevant here: God please grant me the courage to change the things I can, the serenity to accept the things I can't, and the wisdom to know the difference. Living eternally on this earth is not necessarily under our control, but how we live, no matter how long, is much more under our control. It is our responsibility to ourselves and others to maximize how richly we live.

1. What control do you have in your life?

    _____

    _____

    _____

    _____

2. The changes I'm committed to making to live a healthier lifestyle are:

    _____

    _____

    _____

    _____

    _____

    _____

Jerry Duprez

3. The accountability people/factors for these changes are:

_____

_____

_____

_____

4. The impact I want my life to have is:

_____

_____

_____

_____

Revisiting the Valley of the Shadow of Death:

It is presumptuous of any of us to think with certainty we have even tomorrow. As it says in James 4:13-15 (NIV), we really don't know what will happen tomorrow. Nonetheless, what do you think the following decades will be about in your life?

20s:

_____

_____

_____

30s:

_____

_____

_____

40s:

_____

_____

_____

50s:

_____

_____

_____

Jerry Duprez

60s:

_____

_____

_____

70s:

_____

_____

_____

80s:

_____

_____

_____

Methuselah era:

_____

_____

_____

What can you control in your life?

_____

_____

_____

Redemption for One, Healing for Many:

Whether you've lost someone to a criminal act, an accident, a disease, or any other cause, there is an avalanche of questions and emotions that follow. How we deal with these questions and ultimately the pain, will determine the legacy of the lost, as well as potentially your own legacy. We can let bitterness, blame, guilt, denial, or a variety of other things dictate how we carry on after the loss of a loved one. When someone dies, regardless of the manner of their death, the most instinctive human response is to blame someone. Whether it be the person "responsible," God, or anyone else you can think of, this is only a distraction from the pain and ultimately a hindrance to your own healing and ability to move on. I once heard a quote: "Bitterness is like drinking poison and expecting the other person to die." In other words, harboring blame—or guilt, if you're blaming yourself in any way—will end up killing you, one way or another.

1. Who have you lost that's close to you or close to someone you love?

_____

_____

_____

2. If you're honest, do you think you blame someone or something for their death? What about for anything following their death—i.e., insensitivity from family members, unjust circumstances or accusations, etc.?

_____

_____

_____

_____

3. What was the legacy left by the loved one you lost? How might that legacy have been damaged? What can you do to enhance their legacy now?

_____

_____

4. What efforts have been made by others to enhance your loved one's legacy? How have their efforts helped in your healing process?

_____

_____

_____

_____

5. Can you think of any relationships that have been damaged or ended because of circumstances surrounding the death of a loved one? In reflecting on this chapter, are there things you want to do to make amends? How can you go about making this happen?

_____

_____

_____

_____

Jerry Duprez

Overcoming for Us All:

Like I've been saying, we are all faced with many obstacles throughout the course of our lives. These take all different forms and present a variety of challenges for us. In my years of therapy, I have seen countless people who have faced unspeakable tragedies, years of abuse of all types, neglect, abandonment, scarring, and anything else you can imagine. Some survive the worst of it and journey into adulthood as healthy, whole individuals despite the odds, while others who have survived relatively less are fragments of human beings suffering through life. I ask the ones who have seemed to truly overcome and find victory and beauty in the ashes what it was that gave them hope to persevere. The answers are different for each but all similarly allude to an understanding of there being more to life than this earth, more to their experiences than the pain, more to look forward to than more heartache.

1. What are the biggest struggles that come to mind when you look back over your life?

_____

_____

_____

_____

2. Are the majority of these struggles internal or circumstances outside of your control?

_____

_____

_____

_____

3. Considering the first step is awareness, what limits, assumptions, and self-expectations can you identify deep within you?

_____

_____

_____

_____

4. What do you believe these have prevented you from overcoming and/or accomplishing?

_____

_____

_____

_____

Jerry Duprez

5. What things about yourself or your past do you struggle to accept?

_____

_____

_____

_____

6. Do you believe you are responsible for leaving a well-worked out legacy? If yes, to whom do you believe you are responsible? How can you be a steward of this responsibility today?

_____

_____

_____

_____

7. What sources of power do you have to help you overcome?

_____

_____

_____

_____

8. What drives you to overcome? Think about people, causes, and anything else that creates purpose in your life.

_____

_____

_____

Etiology:

My mother-in-law, Millie, is a wonderful, loving person who believes she can control all things, especially related to food and health. Unfortunately, like the rest of us, she will die someday. It is likely, with her way of seeing things, that she will reproach herself horribly for her supposed failures because she will be approaching death as if she's done something wrong that death could even occur. Her behavior regarding her health is very responsible and will result in, very likely, the maximum time for her on this earth. This is the maximum blessing she can give us, at least regarding time with her. But seeing death as a failure versus the natural order of things puts an unrealistic and distorted burden on her that she could free herself of if she could deal with the denial. In any event, we are blessed by her and will both support her behavior and encourage a viewpoint change as she enters her eighties. She is truly a beautiful person.

1. What can I do to live more fully, more in accord with my deepest values?

_____

_____

_____

_____

2. Who are the people I most resent?

_____

_____

_____

_____

_____

_____

_____

_____

_____

3. How can I relieve myself of these resentments?

_____

_____

_____

_____

4. What would "finishing strong" mean to me?

_____

_____

_____

_____

5. What can I do to better prepare for my eventual death?

_____

_____

_____

_____

Jerry Duprez

6. The legacy I want to leave from my life is:

_____

_____

_____

_____

What can I do today to set this up?

_____

_____

_____

_____

_____

_____

_____

_____

_____

7. Do you have resentments toward anyone? List those people below:

_____

_____

_____

_____

What can you do to let those resentments go?

_____

_____

_____

_____

_____

_____

_____

8. If you were to die today, what relationships in your life would have unresolved conflicts, unfinished business, or regrets?

_____

_____

_____

_____

_____

_____

_____

What can you do about that today?

_____

_____

_____

_____

Take the self-test again and compare your scores.

May God bless you and yours.

|LIVE

listen|imagine|view|experience

AUDIO BOOK DOWNLOAD INCLUDED WITH THIS BOOK!

In your hands you hold a complete digital entertainment package. In addition to the paper version, you receive a free download of the audio version of this book. Simply use the code listed below when visiting our website. Once downloaded to your computer, you can listen to the book through your computer's speakers, burn it to an audio CD or save the file to your portable music device (such as Apple's popular iPod) and listen on the go!

How to get your free audio book digital download:

1. Visit www.tatepublishing.com and click on the e|LIVE logo on the home page.
2. Enter the following coupon code:
   667c-560f-c3ae-9c17-b362-54c8-2e9b-b2e4
3. Download the audio book from your e|LIVE digital locker and begin enjoying your new digital entertainment package today!